Software Rules

How the Next Generation of Technology Tools Will
Increase Strategic Effectiveness–and Create
Competitive Advantage

Mark J. Barrenechea

McGraw-Hill

New York   Chicago   San Francisco   Lisbon   London   Madrid   Mexico City   Milan
New Delhi   San Juan   Seoul   Singapore   Sydney   Toronto

McGraw-Hill

A Division of The McGraw-Hill Companies

1234567890 AGM/AGM 098765432

ISBN 0-07-138516-9

Printed and bound by Quebecor World.

McGraw-Hill books are available at special quantity discounts to use as premiums and sales promotions, or for use in corporate training programs. For more information, please write to the Director of Special Sales, Professional Publishing, McGraw-Hill, Two Penn Plaza, New York, NY 10121-2298. Or contact your local bookstore.

This book is printed on recycled, acid-free paper containing a minimum of 50% recycled, de-inked fiber.

Contents

Foreword

Over the past few years, almost every company has made impressive technology investments to cross the Y2K threshold and to ride the first wave of e-business. But now, as pressures to adapt to a changing environment intensify, executives are looking for the return on these investments. The results they expected—in reduced costs or increased revenue—have been painfully slow to materialize.

Frustrated by the outcomes, but clear as to the costs they're incurring, these executives are asking, "So, where's the real business value from all this technology? Much of it seems to have added costs without apparent business benefits."

Increasingly, though, companies are leveraging their technology in new ways. They're creating value by using the software and communications capabilities that enable e-commerce to change the nature of the *interactions* within the organization and between it and its suppliers and customers. The potential savings are enormous.

Interactions—the searching, coordinating, monitoring, and directing that people and organizations do when they exchange goods, services, or ideas—account for over half the labor activity and over a third of all economic activity in the United States. The costs of providing product and pricing information, verifying the status of an order, renewing or modifying a service contract, and similar activities have seemed intractable in the past. However, the low-cost, standards-based technologies that form the Internet and its other manifestations, e.g., intranets and extranets, can dramatically reduce the costs of these and other interactions. These technologies can also enhance the quality and availability of information *about* our interactions—for example, who is buying what products or requesting what information when, or where inventories are in the supply chain. Such information can improve the effectiveness of marketing campaigns, pricing strategies, customer support functions, and a wide variety of operations.

Companies are capturing these kinds of benefits by starting with a clear idea of where they create value, incur costs, and, in so doing, create data. They're using those data to get a clearer picture of the business sooner and to make better decisions. And they are changing their business practices to lower the costs of interactions for themselves, their customers, and their suppliers. Compared to building a new business or a stand-alone Internet channel, doing all this is hard. It requires significant effort, and it challenges the way things are done. And, notwithstanding the potential benefits, these opportunities always seem to come with a big initial price tag for software and systems integration.

In these challenging times, it's hard to sink more money into IT, even for what appear to be valuable undertakings. After several years of freewheeling spending to get ready for Y2K and then scrambling to "create an e-business," senior executives are finding themselves with more complex systems environments than ever, IT budgets that continue to grow faster than revenue, and a litany of related issues that we all thought would be solved by now.

You bought the ERP system, put in the new financials, and upgraded the call-center platform. Your effort to build a unified data warehouse has now spawned multiple data mart projects. And you've spent more than you care to remember to establish a robust e-business channel. Still, you are spending time in management meetings with sales, marketing, and accounting debating the accuracy of customer and revenue data. And every initiative aimed at streamlining processes runs into issues like "those systems don't talk to each other, and it's going to cost a lot of money and take a lot of time to make them do so." Will this ever end?

Mark Barrenechea offers us a provocative way to overcome these evergreen issues and capture the business benefits of technology more rapidly. If you believe that doing things the way you always have but expecting different results is, indeed, one definition of insanity, you will welcome this book. It offers an intriguing vision for technology architecture and a promising remedy for the technology ills that many companies face today.

Will it be hard work to get there? Certainly. Does Mark's vision include a leading role for products and services from Oracle? Yes, but we'd expect no less from a leader of one of the most successful software companies on the planet. In any case, this vision, or something similar, will probably unfold regardless of your choice of software.

If you agree that it's time for a new approach to your technology–and for more coherent solutions, this book is worth your time. It will cause you to think differently, ask different questions, and maybe change your company for the better.

Marc Singer
Coauthor, Net Worth
Principal, McKinsey & Company
San Francisco, California

Preface

Software Rules is a treatment of the need to take what is complex and make it simple, to take what is simple and bring it deep within, to take what is deep within and spread it abroad to embrace business experience and the corporation. The book is about re-creating your business. McGraw-Hill and I have done what we can to blaze the trail and to smooth it out a bit. The rest is up to you.

Mark Barrenechea

Acknowledgments

Bringing this book to market turned on the essential efforts of these people:

Mary Glenn, my editor at McGraw-Hill

David Norton, my friend and adviser

Mark Jarvis of Oracle, an inspiring marketeer (and sometimes buccaneer)

Scott Eldredge, Oracle writer and editor

Oracle's sirens of e-business—*Lisa Arthur, Judy Sim,* and *Karen Tillman*

Steve Miranda for the section "Some Financial Issues" in Chap. 4

Ken Glueck and *Keith Howells,* respectively, for the sections "Government" and "Pharmaceuticals" in Chap. 7

Mike Rosser and *Brad Scott* for their support and their courage to lead change—to jump beyond the "comfort zone"

Dan Rosenberg and *Vicki Huynh,* GUI experts

Oracle employees who contributed to Chap. 7, "Software by Industry"—*Jim Beetem, Andy Bender, Joel Blatt, Robert Brown, Mike Burkett, Tim Cannon, Sam Felix, Leela Koneru, Dave Miner, Hannes Sandmeier, Siva Sundaresan, Wendy Thompson, Lisa Tucci,* and *David Williamson*

Oracle employees who contributed to the appendix, "E-Leaders"—*Richard Abrera, Joe Amerasinghe, Pamela Click, Tarek Fadel, Scott Parsons, Kurt Speck,* and *Shirley Straface*

And the e-leaders themselves:

Dave Ellard, senior vice president of EMC

Debbie Freedman, president, BellSouth Technology Services, Inc.

Bruce Goodman, senior vice president and CIO of Humana

Lori Groves, president of Customer Technologies, Inc. (for BellSouth)

Sean Hickey, CIO, Computing Systems, Embedded & Personal Systems, Hewlett-Packard

Andy Kennedy, vice president, Xerox Information Management—North America Order to Collections

Simon Knight, vice president, Enterprise Systems, IKON

Mike Overly, Global CRM Implementation Manager for Hewlett-Packard

Joe Riera, vice president and CIO of JDS Uniphase

Gary Roberts, Oracle's senior vice president for Global IT

Jason Copeland, who contributed material on contracts

The Oracle E-Business Suite development team, all 4,000 of them

My heartfelt thanks to all.

Mark Barrenechea

Introduction: Shiva's Dance

Flying Blind

The dawn of the 20th century saw the birth of powered flight. Technology honed in World War I spawned the development of civilian aviation, with major U.S. trunk airlines taking shape in the late twenties and early thirties. At that time, aviation was governed by visual flight rules (VFRs), the standards for proceeding from one point to another by visually sighting recognized landmarks on the ground. Powerful rotating light beacons helped pilots find their way from point to point—except when the beacons couldn't be seen because of clouds, fog, or navigation errors. Although airlines had safety rules that forbade flying in inclement weather, weather forecasting was also in its infancy, and pilots often found themselves flying blind. Visionaries saw that airports needed to be connected by a communications infrastructure, and that aircraft needed aids to flight navigation. Safety and efficiency required better information. The year 1929 saw the beginning of instrument flight rules (IFRs). Jimmy Doolittle, an American Army officer, made the first successful instrument flight, using Elmer Sperry's artificial-horizon directional gyroscope to take off, fly a predetermined course, and land—all without visual reference to the earth.

Corporate executives are like pilots constrained to flying under VFRs: hoping to reach an objective, sometimes having to fly blind, and still looking for instruments that can provide the information they need to steer the course they want. Executives need information like the information pilots can get from their instruments: information that is precise, prompt, well organized, and reliable. For a pilot, seconds can make the difference between a smooth flight and serious trouble. That's not true for a corporate executive, you may say. Would you bet on it?

Suppose the CEO of XYZ Corp. reads an article in the *Wall Street Journal* Tuesday morning that convinces him that demand for XYZ's products is going to drop significantly over the year to come. How soon does he want to take action? And how long is he willing to wait before the company begins to respond to his direction?

Instrument Flying

Even in these days of depressed business activity, companies are spending a lot of money on software. Top executives sometimes spend hundreds of millions of dollars on licenses for software that they will never see in use. There's no way that this makes any sense—except historically. The humblest and most routine jobs—data entry, bookkeeping, and the like—have always been the easiest to automate, for the same reason that doing them has always required the least training and expertise. But the idea that a data-entry clerk for XYZ Corp. needs the help of business software more than XYZ's CEO does is crazy. The more complex and difficult a job is, the greater the value of automating that job, in whole or in part. The challenge is to do so constructively.

Remember Deep Blue? Its 1997 triumph over world chess champion Gary Kasparov was a stunning triumph for software, and its architects were justly proud. But—if they wanted a *serious* challenge—they could have tried programming a computer to learn English as well in four years, by speaking it and hearing it spoken, as an average American child does. Then they (or more likely a later generation of computer scientists) could move on to programming a computer to run a business.

Meanwhile, computers are being programmed to *help* run businesses, and the chief officers of businesses are the people who need that help the most, if only because the decisions they're making are the most important. Competition among software vendors is pushing those vendors inexorably toward automating what has never before been automated, and the difficulties of getting it right are offset by the potential prize—to be recognized, and rewarded, for helping corporate leadership, not "just" corporations, to be more cost-effective and more successful.

But corporate leaders need to attend to advanced business software not merely because that software can give them more insight and more control from their own desktops. Fundamental changes are under way in business software, and they span the entire range of corporate activity. The most important of all is the long march of consolidation, with its two outstanding effects: (1) to reduce the number of vendors; and (2) to make more comprehensive the functionality offered (and integrated, to one extent or another) by each of the vendors that survive. As vendors' offerings grow more comprehensive, the degree to which each is internally integrated is likely to rise: even those customers that are willing to go on paying large sums to consultants to integrate applications from diverse vendors are going to lose patience rapidly if offerings from *one* vendor still need to be integrated with one another.

As a result, business software will morph increasingly from an industry of parts and labor into one of finished goods. Vendors will spend more time and money integrating their products, whereas customers will spend less. To reduce their own costs, vendors will try to integrate their own products once only, in such a way as to serve the greatest number of customers. The effect will be to slash the total cost of ownership for customers, but to do so in a way that deprives those customers of a measure of flexibility. The Gartner Group estimates that the crowd of customer relationship management (CRM) software vendors will shrink from the current 200 to about 50 by 2004. Clearly, the range of choices for a purchaser is likely to contract, by some measures. The vendors that emerge from the coming shakeout can—and must—combat this trend by building applications that are more—and more easily—configurable.

Crucial to integration—within vendors' offerings and between them—is the use of a single database with a single schema. Crucial too is the smooth automation of complete business flows or processes, building on the single schema to minimize (ideally, to eliminate) human involvement in every process in which such involvement is not essential. Granted, marketing teams and sales reps may be irreplaceable; as a rule, though, data-entry clerks, telephone operators, COBOL programmers, and many others are not. Business software needs to press forward with its mission: to shift the burden of work from carbon-based to silicon-based intelligence.

The Awful Truth

The awful truth has emerged: The Internet is not going to solve all the world's problems.

But it *will* solve some of them, and it is profoundly transforming the way in which companies do business. Will the transformation increase the profitability of the typical business? Who knows? But it will certainly confer a competitive advantage on the companies that first complete that transformation. It will empower business executives to implement their strategic decisions much more rapidly than has ever before been possible.

Traditionally, major corporations have been like 747s, coming about slowly and ponderously once they begin to bank. To compete effectively, they must become more like hummingbirds, able to accelerate instantly in any direction. Internet software can never ensure that executives will make sound business decisions, but it can give them much-needed leverage by enabling them to put their decisions into effect in short order—and to reverse them just as rapidly if they go awry.

This does not imply greater profitability for Internet-adept companies. Does General Electric achieve a greater ROI than the British East India Company? Is Microsoft more profitable than Standard Oil? The questions are irrelevant. What is clear is that the greatest benefits of the Internet will ultimately accrue to consumers, because every company will go right on competing to provide its customers with a better deal than they can get from its competitors.

For the companies that first master the art of Internet business, the principal reward will be that they'll get to go on doing it. In many cases, this reward will come at the expense of competitors that come around later and do so with less skill, foresight, and industry—or luck. Those competitors will find themselves outmaneuvered, like a crow mobbed by songbirds.

Simple ∴ Rapid

How will the new maneuverability be achieved? By simplicity.

It's not that business systems will ever be inherently simple. The technology that merely keeps the Internet running—forget about what Company XYZ may want to use it for—is mind-numbingly complex. International corporate strategy is more byzantine and far more important than any game of chess. The challenge for 21st-century businesses, and for the software vendors that support them, is to buffer the human beings involved from the complications—to make it *seem* easy, like Willie Mays pulling down a fly to deep center field at the Polo Grounds.

The whole point of software is to take over mental work from humans—freeing them to do what? More mental work. (Don't worry: There'll always be more left than people really want to do.) The mental work that people do has always varied in complexity and importance, and the software industry has always weighed these two attributes in deciding which areas to attack next. In the world of business, the back office was the first target; it was generally recognized that business functions relating directly to customers were typically more various and more sensitive, and only over the last few years has CRM software truly come into its own. We have arrived at a point where every area of business functionality has been automated—to some degree.

The use of software to sift out the complexities that it can address constructively means that executives now command a lot of inanimate help in making their business decisions, whether those decisions are tactical or strategic. Business decisions no longer need to be based on hours of tedious calculations done manually—or on intuitions about the marketplace. What used to be mere business facts have evolved progressively into business information and business intelligence. The systems that enable this evolution are not intended to make top-level business decisions, but they *are* intended to arm executives with the analytical intelligence that will enable *them* to make those decisions reliably and to champion them effectively.

Business software was rising to this challenge when the Internet was still hull down on the horizon. But the Internet will prove to be the greatest force for simplification that American business has ever seen. Because of the Internet, Company XYZ can now run all its computer systems from a single information technology (IT) installation, and by so doing can ensure that those systems are internally coherent and present a single well-organized and homogeneous face to their users, whether those users are employees, customers, investors, or business partners. It can provide its top executives with a comprehensive view of what all the corporate departments are up to, giving them unprecedented understanding and control of the business.

Even more important, the Internet enables companies to interact much more extensively with one another; but, because it does so, it dangles before them an irresistible incentive to align their computer systems for mutual intelligibility. The benefits they foresee from such alignment are driving the development and adoption of a wide range of Internet-related technical standards, but that is only the beginning. As time passes, the same incentive will pressure them to simplify and standardize their internal systems, to progressively eliminate company-specific peculiarities in business processes, and thus to rely more and more fully on uncustomized industry-standard software.

So, if we're making all this progress, why is American business still in the doldrums?

Where Wall Street Intersects the I-Bahn

What has the Internet done to the stock markets?

The Internet was by far the most powerful force behind the rise of the NASDAQ Composite Index from 1343.87 (on October 8, 1998) to 5132.52 (on March 10, 2000) and its subsequent fall to 1387.06 (on September 21, 2001). Annualized, the rise was 257 percent, the decline was −57.4 percent,[1] and the advance from the earlier to the later minimum was 1.1 percent. At the close of trading on September 21, 2001, the Comp was 72.3 percent off its high.

Meanwhile the Dow Jones Industrial Average remained essentially static. This is because the investment community has been alive to the implications of the Internet for high-tech companies but has not understood its potential to transfigure the operations of more traditional enterprises. Now that the immense Internet hype has been painfully deflated, we shall see the major indexes rise, roughly in proportion to the true value of the services that the Net makes possible. These rises will be impressive, but this time we'll see the valuations of traditional companies growing too.

The Great Crash

On September 3, 1929, the Dow Jones Industrial Average reached a peak of 386.10. Then, for 50 days, it fluctuated between that figure

---

[1] In annualized terms, the decline from the peak to the low of April 4, 2001, was greater, at −66.5 percent.

and 303.80, touching the lower level on October 23. On October 24 it closed at 299.50, but this disguised an intraday fall to 272.30; the 11 percent plunge, though followed by a rapid recovery, was a portent recognized by few at the time.

October 29 is famous as "Black Tuesday," the day of panic on Wall Street—but ironically so. It saw the DJIA drop 11.7 percent, but the index had dropped farther—12.8 percent—the day before. Moreover, by the close of Halloween it had more than made up for its big loss on October 29. What distinguished October 29 was the volume of activity, which was enormous for the time: 16.5 million shares changed hands.

Still, it took more than Black Tuesday to make the Great Crash. The DJIA continued its decline for almost three years, bottoming at 40.60 on July 8, 1932. At this level, the index reflected the loss of 89.5 percent of the nominal value of the stocks it included. The DJIA then began a recovery, but it did not surpass its 1929 peak until November 24, 1954—a quarter-century after it had first reached that height.[2] The recovery period saw the index rise more slowly than its overall historical rate, probably reflecting a lasting distrust among investors and ex-investors, and the NYSE did not break the Black Tuesday volume record until 1968. A lot of cash spent a lot of time hidden under mattresses.

The Dot Bomb

During the 18 months from March 2000 to September 2001, the NASDAQ Composite Index has surpassed the catastrophic record set by the DJIA. From a high of 5132.52 on March 10, 2000, it dropped as low as 1387.06 on September 21, 2001, marking the loss of more than 72 percent of the value that it represented at its height. This is the greatest drop in our lifetimes for a major American stock index, and corporate shares around the world have lost a total value of roughly $12 trillion. The plunge, though not proportionally as great as that of the DJIA in 1929–1932, has been steeper. But we haven't heard reports of investors flinging themselves out of windows.

At least, not yet. Following the terrorist disaster of September 11, 2001, the NASDAQ Composite is at last showing modest signs of a

---

[2]And it must have seemed even longer to investors, because the market was active six days a week until June 1952.

possible recovery; in mid-October it stands fully 24 percent *below* the DJIA's corresponding level 583 days after its 1929 peak. In other respects, the plots of the two declines are frighteningly similar thus far (Fig. I-1). In the figure, all DJIA closing levels for 1929–1932 have been multiplied by a constant such that the DJIA peak equals the NASDAQ peak. Both plots begin 69 days before the peak day, and the x-axis is calibrated in calendar days.

The big difference, of course, is that the NASDAQ debacle has not been accompanied by a depression. Even the recently confirmed recession is still shallow. The absence, thus far, of really grave problems for the economy is reflected by the fact that the DJIA itself remained largely static for 31 months.[3] If the NASDAQ plunge has a meaning for the economy as a whole, that meaning has not yet been identified. What the plunge clearly *does* mean is a repudiation of the stratospheric price/earnings (P/E) ratios that used to be carried by

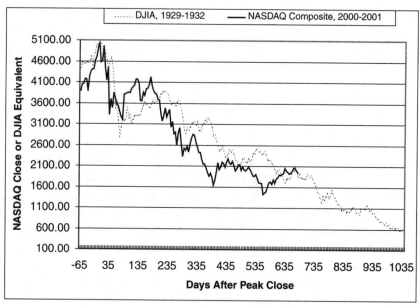

Figure I-1. The Great Crash Compared to the NASDAQ Plunge

[3]During which period it was always within 12.6 percent of 10,414. That streak was interrupted—it sank to 14.3 percent below—on the first trading day after the terrorist attack on the World Trade Center and the Pentagon. But by October 3, 2001, it was back within the earlier range.

hundreds of high-tech companies—P/E ratios that had to be expressed as absolute values to accommodate the horde of dot-coms, and others, whose earnings never rose as high as zero.

The Internet—or, more accurately, its enthusiasts—bears much of the responsibility for the NASDAQ crash. But this new technology, though its initial promise has been tarnished, has done nothing more for investors than to repeat a pattern set by earlier revolutionary innovations, including the railroad and the motorcar. Each led to grossly inflated optimism as to its effect on the world of business; yet, while the waves of optimism were rising and falling, the revolutions were pressing forward.

Creative Destruction

1   Venture-capital firms invest in high-tech start-ups. This may recur for several rounds.

2   High-tech companies develop products and services and market them to customer companies—and sometimes directly to consumers.

3   Customer and other companies often invest in high-tech start-ups.

4   If it survives long enough, the typical start-up eventually executes an initial public offering (IPO). Cash flows in from the investing public in exchange for shares issued by the company, and in some cases for shares already held by venture-capital firms. Some start-ups eventually do secondary and possibly later stock offerings.

The stock markets, and the businesses whose shares are traded in them, are manifestations of Shiva's dance of creative destruction.[4] Wealth is created and destroyed by the businesses, created and destroyed by the markets; and, as with life itself, nobody can say to what extent the creation or the destruction is a mere illusion. Many of the processes that were at work in the dot-com boom and its aftermath are illustrated in Figure I-2.

The figure is somewhat simplified, since it omits (for instance) flows of cash and shares between venture capitalists and non-high-tech companies. But it does show most of the processes that concern us here. During the period since the NASDAQ hit its all-time high, there have been massive net outflows from venture capitalists and

---

[4] To use Schumpeter's phrase.

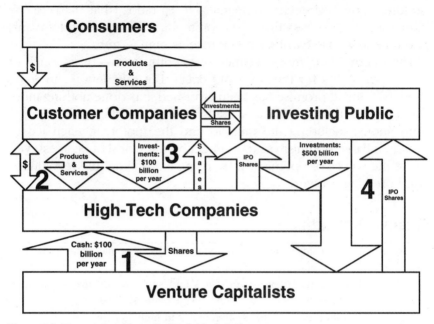

Figure I-2. Transaction Flows in High-Tech Industry

the investing public, while high-tech companies have been a sink. (Cash-flow estimates, where provided, are courtesy of Bob Cringely;[5] they pertain to the period leading up to March 10, 2000.) This is not to say that high-tech companies have realized net inflows; instead, cash coming into them has been flushed down drains not shown in the figure—mostly spent on services, staff, real estate, and equipment from which the companies could not wring a profit.

Almost everybody got carried away by the hype surrounding the Internet. What this meant, specifically, was much disproportionate enthusiasm about the business prospects for various new products and services closely tied to the Net. Contagious optimism spread from would-be entrepreneurs to venture capitalists, and from both groups to the investing public.

New ventures were founded on such unsound business plans because of the general delusion that the Internet conferred the Midas touch. This meant that capital was diverted from sound business

---

[5]"Cargo Cult," April 27, 2001, at www.pbs.org/cringely/pulpit/pulpit20010426.html.

plans that had no Internet focus, and this meant, in turn, that a great deal of ingenuity was expended in trying to identify the 273rd-best Internet business plan that might have turned more constructively to trying to identify the fourth-best non-Internet business plan. Creation itself clustered around the Net, while nemesis dogged the business plans that neglected to mention the magic word.

But the contagion slowed dramatically as it advanced toward customer companies and consumers, which evidently concluded that a lot of the new products and services on offer were not worth the prices being asked. Pet food shipped cross-country? Grocery delivery by vans?

The rapid deflation of the NASDAQ reversed the situation. Now the great majority of Internet-based business plans came to be viewed as having trivial value or none at all, and high-tech companies that had peddled their wares to the dot-coms were suddenly recognized as having futures much less rosy than had been imagined. The reversal was effectively a confession of error by Internet fanatics, and for that confession a penance has been imposed. Venture capitalists, the investing public, and companies that held positions in dot-coms and the like all feel impoverished, if not aggrieved, and the result is a general drying up of capital for investment in new business ideas of any kind. (Venture capital funding, according to a Reuters article,[6] shrank from $26.7 billion in the first quarter of 2000 to $11.7 billion in the corresponding quarter of 2001.) Moreover, many corporations, especially in high tech, have seen their market capitalizations slashed by 60 or 70 percent, which makes them loath to use their stock to acquire, or even to invest in, other companies. Some tried to drive their own business by extending credit to dot-coms that later went under; they are not eager to repeat that experience. The gross effect is to discourage innovation and the entrepreneurial spirit.

Yet this effect is offset to some extent by another. Shiva's heel has crushed the dot-coms, and their corpses now litter the landscape. The destruction of the wealth that they diverted from sounder business ideas and directed to staff and equipment that were destined never to produce anything of much value is largely finished. The said staff and equipment are being released in large numbers from their unprofitable undertakings and are again at the disposal of the

---

[6]Ilaina Jonas, "Software Mergers—Fewer, Cheaper, Choosier," May 13, 2001.

marketplace, which has the usual option of dedicating them to generating revenue. So are hundreds of executives who might have retired on the basis of their stock holdings—before the value of those holdings collapsed. Anyone and anything that is not now in use may well be employed one day by the larger and sounder technology companies—those that have the resources to weather the downturn and even to buy out many of the smaller failing enterprises.

This process causes a lot of pain as people lose their jobs and their fortunes, and as slightly used equipment floods the marketplace, creating inventory problems for manufacturers. But the economy can only gain, in the long run, from the opportunity to redirect resources that were formerly employed in cloud-cuckoo-land.[7]

The recovery of the NASDAQ Composite Index, which is presumably under way at last, is certain to proceed much more sedately than its earlier rise beyond 5000. As in the Great Crash, investors have been burned, and they will prove much more cautious for years to come. Yet, if the index can again rise at its average rate since January 1985, it will take "only" another 10 years—not 25—for it to surpass its high-water mark of the year 2000.

Rapid Response

Will it do so? Probably. Some readers will groan to hear me say that the principal reason is the Internet, but this is nevertheless the truth. Indeed, if the investment community had focused from the start on the Internet's value to existing businesses, not on how the Net was going to transmute every start-up with an Internet-related business plan, the year 2000 might have witnessed neither the prodigious run-up in the NASDAQ nor the ensuing deflation.

Although a great deal of software for Internet applications already exists, the great bulk of what businesses need in order to complete the revolution has yet to be written. What is needed above all is software to optimize the supply and demand chains—together. Though we've heard a great deal in recent months about supply chain management (SCM), the consensus is that supply-chain processes are far more complex and subtle than anything that

---

[7]As in Aristophanes' *Clouds.*

existing applications can support. As for demand chain management, the term has hardly been heard;[8] but the challenges, and the potential rewards, are comparable to those for SCM.

What such software can accomplish will depend heavily on the degree of uniformity that businesses can attain, both internally and around the business world. Business efficiency can be maximized by uniform messaging conventions, by uniform terms and conditions, by uniform business processes. Before the Internet, businesses were much more introverted than they can now afford to be; the Internet, by encouraging interbusiness communication, pushes businesses inexorably toward the adoption of uniform standards. These, in turn, will facilitate corporate flexibility and rapidity of response.

Moreover, businesses have hundreds of billions of dollars to gain by improving the efficiency of their IT operations. Again, the major opportunities in this area are enabled by the Internet; because they are both more obvious and less daunting conceptually than demand- and supply-chain enhancements, they represent a much more likely source of near-term improvement in margins. This book draws upon the experiences of eight businesses that are leading the e-revolution: BellSouth, EMC, Hewlett-Packard, Humana, IKON, JDS Uniphase, Oracle, and Xerox. Each has a unique story.

The goal is simplification—for rapid response. Strategic corporate decisions must be based on fact; corporate systems must assemble, interpret, and present the facts effectively to support the decision-making process. But our focus here is on what it takes to minimize the interval between the moment the executive decision is made and its full implementation within the corporate systems. This interval will be the center of attention in the end game for the rapid-response enterprise and the software vendors contending for that enterprise's business. The simplicity and uniformity made possible by the Internet will impel the final wave of the Information Revolution.

Declaration of Interest

Because I'm working at Oracle, it's inevitable that I'll be writing from the Oracle perspective. We at Oracle believe passionately that every

---

[8]An Internet search using AltaVista returns about 25 hits on "supply chain management" for every 1 on "demand chain management."

business needs a single database with a single schema, and business processes that are automated and integrated from start to finish. Most companies' current business processes are fragmented, isolated, and incomplete. The responsibility of corporate chief executives is not to understand such business processes but to recognize their deficiencies and to figure out how to get away from them. The destination of choice is integration that spans not only broad ranges of functionality but varying depths of technology—not integration that begins with divergent products and seeks the least inefficient way to coordinate them, but integration that is designed into the product.

Oracle is the world leader in database science, so it has a clear interest in promoting solid and coordinated data as the logical basis for e-business. The company also markets the Oracle E-Business Suite, the purpose of which is to organize, integrate, and empower customer businesses in the ways set forth in this book. Readers need to bear in mind that Oracle competitors are marketing products with similar purposes; prospective purchasers will want to make allowances as they judge appropriate for any relevant claims that I advance.

Mark J. Barrenechea
Berkeley, California

1

Business Nirvana

Business executives have been through the wringer. They have survived the era of the client/server configuration, which was born with one node in a grave that was being dug, even then, by the Internet. They have survived the dreaded Y2K, a year or two of hype followed by all the drama of frozen nitro. They have scaled the heights of the Internet boom and plumbed the depths of the Internet bust. They are ready for less interesting times.

Business nirvana . . . what would that be like?

The four measures of corporate success are market share, revenue, cash flow, and profitability. Every company's senior executives need to assess each of these and to steer the company toward the desired combination. They need rapid response, made possible by software that supports such assessments, that enables sensitive adjustments to the course they are steering, and that generates prompt and reliable feedback as to the effects of each adjustment. Little time must be lost between their business decisions and the implementation of those decisions in the corporate systems.

The relative weights accorded to these four measures will vary among industries, among companies within an industry, and sometimes among divisions of a company. Currently, characteristic variations among industries include

- Automobile manufacturers seeking profitability
- Pharmaceutical companies contesting market share
- CPG (consumer packaged goods) companies driving cash flow

- High-tech companies optimizing margins
- Yahoo! and Amazon driving revenue

Next, to sketch out nirvana in more operational terms:

- Management would be armed to take full control of the business. Such control has long been impossible for multinational companies, which have typically relied on multiple client/server systems (one per country, each isolated from the others).
- Comprehensive and subtle business information would promote an evolution toward management by fact, not by force of personality—thus harmonizing executive teams.
- Business vitality would brush aside traditional limits to growth, enabling businesses to scale without obvious limits and to operate globally.
- Change would become the norm, happening so smoothly that it would be welcomed by a business's stakeholder community—its employees, customers, suppliers, and partners—and happening so quickly that some of the old guard would view it as reckless. Stasis would emerge as the real enemy.
- The management and implementation of change would centralize within the corporation and thus gain strategic value.
- A majority of all stakeholder activity would consist of self-service transactions, which participants could engage in from any point on the globe and at any time of any day of the week.
- Product introductions and upgrades would be global, covering all lines of business, business partners, and supply-chain sources; each would take place during a weekend.
- Marketing automation would evolve into electronic selling.
- Direct sales and service organizations would shrink, being displaced in large part by electronic sales and service.
- Nevertheless, human staff would represent the business at all reasonable times; for global enterprises, this would mean 8×7 representation rolling from each of three or four centers distributed around the world to the next, thus covering the clock dial. (For example, such centers might be located in Omaha, Sydney, Bombay, and London.)

- Expenses would be lowered across a wide range:
  - General and administrative expenses would drop dramatically.
  - Data centers would be reduced in size and/or number.
  - Larger computers would increasingly be replaced by smaller ones.
  - Data-center staff would be reduced.
  - Other infrastructure costs would be reduced.
  - Customization costs would be reduced.

- Supply chains would be pervasively optimized. Demand chains would be established.

- Mass customization (build-to-order) would become a reality.

- Margins would increase significantly, approaching the maxima theoretically attainable.

- Customer satisfaction would increase.

- Executives could focus on core business competencies; they would no longer need to be—or to employ—computer hobbyists.

Something very close to this state of affairs will become attainable over the next ten years. Software will make it possible. The subject of this book is the nature and impact of the software required: the rules of software, and the software that will rule.

The argument of the book is segmented as follows:

- Businesses must wage war on complexity, both in systems and in business processes.

- The focus of business software is moving away from the automation of discrete functions toward the automation of logically complete business flows.

- The advent of the Internet means that every business now has an incentive to understand and to respond to global markets, to operate on a 24×7 basis, and to leverage its human capital to the hilt in serving its stakeholders.

- Customer self-service, the centralization of change management, and the reduction and concentration of computer systems, all facilitated by the Internet, promote the collection and deployment of business intelligence, leading to increased management by fact.

- Software is and must remain to some degree industry-specific.

- Case study after case study shows that businesses can save thousands, millions, or even billions of dollars through productivity heightened by the use of strategic software.

- Software is metamorphosing into online services more rapidly than most imagine: for small businesses, for big businesses—for all businesses.

Let's call this Vision 1. Is it outlandish? Compare it to Vision 2:

Imagine an America in which all cities are connected by great paved highways; standard automobiles, with standard parts and fuel, enable Americans to travel freely and with confidence from Boston to San Francisco. Businesses can move goods and labor freely. Produce from California can be sold on Beacon Hill, Maine lobsters in Berkeley.

At the dawn of the 20th century, this would have been nearly unimaginable. In 1903 a Winton became the first car to struggle across the country from one coast to the other, chugging for 63 days through mud, across cobblestones, along corduroy roads, across unpaved deserts, over mountains. The horse was a more reliable means of transportation, and the airplane was still no more than a figment of many imaginations. In 1919, as a young army officer, Dwight Eisenhower took part in the first transcontinental convoy, which (still) took almost two months to get from Washington, D.C., to San Francisco. This experience, together with his later glimpse of the advanced autobahns of Germany, sowed the seeds of the Interstate Highway System, which Eisenhower signed into law in 1956.

To realize Vision 2, many fundamental changes were essential:

1. From the horse to the car

2. To standardization of parts

3. To assembly-line manufacturing

4. To greater centralization of manufacturing

5. To vastly increased production, standardization, and distribution of gasoline

6. From cash purchases to installment loans

7. From dirt roads to a massive interstate highway system

8. To standardization of service, including tools, skills, and training

This list involves a lot of shorthand. For instance, changing from the horse to the car meant overcoming extensive legal resistance:

because the earliest cars frightened horses, many states and localities passed laws impeding the normal operation of automobiles—and some of these laws are still on the books. Items 2, 3, 4, and 6 were essential because, in turn-of-the-20th-century America, even the least expensive automobile cost twice the average annual salary, and that price excluded headlights, bumpers, carburetors, and the like, all of which had to be purchased as add-ons.

The transformations required at the start of the 21st century to realize Vision 1 appear perhaps less daunting. But if this is so, it is because a great deal of work was done in the 20th century to develop the infrastructure that makes the vision imaginable. Most important, this infrastructure included the nationwide telephone system, which was largely completed during the first quarter of the century, and the Internet, which was begun in the century's third quarter and is still under rapid development. Smaller, but still crucial, were the recent development of the World Wide Web (WWW) and of WWW browsers, both of which made the Internet easier to use.

Many of the transformations needed to enable rapid response are now under way within the *Fortune* 5000:

Area	From	To
Administration	Traditional	Self-service
Automation	Isolated functions	Complete business flows
Back- and front-office processes	Segregated	Integrated
Business processes	Complex	Simplified
Business-to-business (B2B) relationships	Isolation	Collaboration
Channels	High-cost	Low-cost (electronic)
Information	Business data	Business intelligence
Operations	Local	Global
Software	Parts and labor	Finished goods: comprehensive e-business suites
	Generic	Industry-oriented
	Distributed products	Services
Software, implementation of	As customized	As issued
Workweeks	40-hour (8 × 5)	168-hour (24 × 7), globally segmented

Once these transformations are complete, how will business be done?

Say you're about to introduce a new product. You mine your global database for customers and prospects who are likely to be interested, extracting names first for a control group, then for regional groups, and finally for an exhaustive list. As a vehicle for the global launch, you design a marketing campaign marshaling telesales, direct mail, e-mail, and print and Internet-based ads. You alert your business partners and communicate the news throughout your supply chain: Heads up! Big demand is on its way!

The campaign takes off: e-mails with quotes and collateral are sent to your existing customers and to prospects drawn from third-party lists. Interested parties visit your Web site for demos, for references, and to communicate with other customers online. Purchases take place through your global Web store, through telesales, and in response to orders placed by field sales agents and by partners. Customers and prospects use automated tools to configure the product to their specific needs, then check its availability. Telesales agents use Web-based collaboration to help close business. Orders are filled from geographically appropriate locations.

And suddenly you run out of parts! Now your supply chain kicks into action, finding vendors to fill the demand—fast, reliably, and with high quality. Using automation, contracts are written, renewed, enhanced, and merged. Customers come to your Web site for training, customer service, threaded discussions, order status, and perhaps for returns.

During the entire process, you account financially for all these activities automatically, paying sales reps, support agents, and partners. Employees use self-service applications to handle their benefits, expenses, and travel-related services. Customers are involved, suppliers paid, partners rewarded.

Oh, and you did this product introduction globally, in 100 countries, meeting distinct localization requirements in each—requirements like the serialization of invoice numbers and translation of contract details. All stages in the process are interconnected through wireless and mobile communications, through conventional phones, through TV, and through the Web.

Want to drive from Boston to San Francisco?

This level of automation will be delivered within five years by out-of-the-box software from one or more large software companies, and it will have been deployed by as many as half of the *Fortune* 5000. This will mean a major advance in these companies' competitive abilities. More important, it will spell the end of the last major chapter of the industrial revolution, because businesses will be closing in on maximum automation and optimal efficiency. The information age will have matured. "Data in, information out" will be the rule of the day.

It used to be said that IBM was not so much a company one competed with as the environment in which everybody competed. Analogously, suites of e-business software will define the competitive environment of the near future. They will make possible the emergence of the rapid-response enterprise.

2

The War on Complexity

Automobiles and Automation

Software has emerged as the most important industry on earth. Without software, armies cannot fight, bankers bank, CEOs direct, doctors operate, engineers build, financiers invest, governments tax. True, we have engineered our dependence on software, but we have done so willingly. Now software is necessary: for groceries to reach supermarkets, for benefits checks to reach veterans, for Social Security checks to reach the elderly. Software keeps our cars and trains running and our planes flying, and it makes them safe. It keeps electricity flowing through the power grid—and it consumes its fair share. It keeps our water running—and the Internet.

Software has produced the world's most highly capitalized companies, many of its most successful companies, and many of its richest men and women. Status approaching that of movie stars has been won by some of the titans of the industry—Andreessen, Barksdale, Bezos, Case, Dell, Ellison, Gates, Gerstner, Jobs, McNealy, and more. Software is the sun of the information age. Banish software, and banish all the world.

The software industry is uniquely American, and posterity will judge it to be the greatest American achievement of the 20th century—and of the 21st.[1] But software as we know it is not yet 60 years of age. As a

---

[1]One major non-American software company still survives: SAP. But, like many of its fallen comrades, SAP proved bewilderingly slow to answer the challenge of business-software integration in the age of the Internet. It seems recently to have recovered its balance.

discipline, it is unnervingly immature. Indeed, its immaturity resonates with the sheer *Americanness* of the software enterprise. Software has only begun to scale heights that will prove Himalayan. We stand now like climbers at Everest Base Camp, looking up perilous slopes toward the dead zone.

In what way is the software business immature? It is an industry of parts and labor; its challenge now is to ripen into an industry of finished goods. In the past, any business that sought to automate the full range of its operations was compelled to use disparate software products from multiple vendors and to invest the necessary time and effort to integrate them to some passable degree—meaning, in some cases, not at all. The undeniable complexity of the operation of large business enterprises has been conceded by hundreds of vendors, each of which has chosen to focus on one or another specific area of operations: many products that have emerged have optimized the automation of such local areas, but their boundaries sometimes abut on voids and sometimes on alien applications that speak foreign languages. Business applications from disparate vendors are city-states, not at war with their neighbors but abiding by the terms of an uneasy truce. The result has been not to simplify but to further complicate the business landscape, some of the oddest features of which are paradoxes: the more a company spends on information technology, the less valuable the results; the more databases a company maintains, the less business intelligence it can marshal.[2]

Compare this to the situation in the automobile industry, which also has materials, parts, labor, and service. Nobody who wants a car follows the "best of breed" approach, buying the engine from BMW, the transmission from Nissan, the fuel-injection system from Ferrari, the tires from Michelin, and the finish from Ford. Nobody hires Andersen Consulting to weld the parts together; even for a hobbyist to assemble an entire car this way is almost unheard of. If cars were produced this way, they would be too expensive to buy, would take too long to deliver, and would cost too much to maintain. Every car would be unique, not only in its personalization but in its basic components; all the benefits of mass production would be lost. Suppose Ferrari were to upgrade its fuel-injection system: would it confer with BMW and Nissan to ensure that its new

[2]This is Ellison's Law.

system would match the next versions of the engine and transmission? Or would Implementation Business Mechanics have to stand by to undertake the upgrade and to service and maintain every "best of breed" car? This time, next time, every time?

The software industry today is like the auto industry in the last few years.[3] Before 1912, the typical car company purchased most of the major auto components from parts manufacturers and integrated those parts into automobiles. And fifty companies a year were entering the auto-manufacturing business. (Sound familiar?)

Henry Ford was the first to recognize that the "best of breed" approach does not scale. Under his leadership, the manufacturing process was gradually concentrated, with his model of vertical integration culminating in the 2000-acre River Rouge plant in the 1920s. When the last Model T rolled off the assembly line in 1927, more than half of the cars on the country's roads were Fords. Though the number of manufacturers has steadily declined since then, the consumer still has enormous breadth of choice, and quality—even quality per cost—has risen without interruption.

A similar evolution has begun in the business software industry. It began in the early 1990s with the coming of age of the World Wide Web, which is crucial for the integration of the operations of any multinational corporation—and even more so for the corporation's coordination with the operations of its suppliers, consumers, and business partners. Thousands of companies have developed business applications that exploit the connectivity provided by the Web; proportionally, only a few have been moving toward extensive suites of software designed to Web-enable and integrate entire business areas.

Such suites seek to simplify both the automation of business practices and the practices themselves, empowering executives to take control of their businesses. They generate business intelligence that can help executives to manage by force of fact, rather than by force of personality, with the upshot that managerial conflict is reduced. And the economies they enable are potentially mind-boggling. Yet, even now, it is too early to grasp the full potential of this revolution. Once all the business data are brought together and

---

[3]Before Ford (more precisely, before the Model T). A tip of the hat to Aldous Huxley.

reconciled, once the most effective processes are in place and the most revelatory business intelligence is operating, what efficiencies, what innovations will be possible?

Business software has the potential to spin $1 trillion a year in revenues. Competition for that prize will be in proportion to its magnitude. But, as with the auto industry, as with the PC retail business, as with the Internet marketplace, the number of companies that will survive to compete is bound to shrink. The companies that are first to market with e-business suites are likely not only to survive but to thrive. They will be joined by others. And the marketplace will begin to prune.

As number 1 of *The 22 Immutable Laws of Marketing* states,[4] "It's better to be first than it is to be better." Ideally, of course, a company's offering would be better in the second respect as well as in the first. Compared with the products of leading vendors of point solutions for business software, e-business suites may not offer every feature a customer desires, although some will offer every feature the customer needs. But to make such comparisons is to miss the point about point solutions: they will not answer the greatest challenge facing businesses today, which is to integrate and coordinate the business's full range of software operations. Companies operate according to business flows, and many business flows cannot be complete without the support of two, three, or four—or more— applications from multiple point-solution vendors. Inevitably, the suite approach is simpler to implement and simpler to understand and operate with regard to business data and processes.

Not everybody will be pleased with the advent of e-business suites. Industry analysts would be happy with an arena full of equally armed gladiators. With the death or enfeeblement of so many former competitors—Ashton-Tate, Baan, BMC, Borland, Claris, Lotus, the Mac OS, McCormick & Dodge, OS/2, Prime, Sperry Rand, WordPerfect— these analysts have increasingly had to fall back on Microsoft's earnings, sins, and strategies for their subject matter. They are not in a mood to welcome more consolidation. More important, system implementers are unhappy. King's ransoms have flowed into their pockets in return for their work in software evaluation, procurement,

---

[4]Al Ries and Jack Trout, *The 22 Immutable Laws of Marketing* (New York: HarperBusiness, 1993).

implementation, and maintenance; now they see their livelihoods hanging in the balance.

My vision implies that the orientation of system implementers will change. Once an e-business suite is functionally complete, it is not rational for system implementers to work to "integrate" it or to extend its functionality. In relation to their customers, the implementers' position should align with that of the software vendors: their opening move is to challenge each customer to demonstrate that the customer truly needs e-business functionality that is either absent from the suite being used or not well integrated within it. If the customer so demonstrates, the implementer may take short-term action to address the e-business need; but in the long term it is the vendor's responsibility to make sure that all needed functionality is built in.

Thus the work of system implementers is likely, over time, to become less technical and more strategic. They will continue to be involved in the setup and implementation of software, but vendors will be working continuously to minimize the need to modify that software. Implementers' *raison d'être* will move toward business process reengineering, an activity that—because it addresses higher strategic levels—is potentially of much greater value to the customer.

The War on Complexity

"**complex** . . . *adj, sometimes* –er/-est [L *complexus*, past part. of *complecti* to entwine around, embrace, fr. *com-* + *plectere* to braid — more at ply]."[5]

Etymology does not reliably help us to understand the meaning of a word, but in this case the derivation is unusually eloquent. Stemming from a verb meaning "to braid," *complexity* inherits the concept of multiplicity—specifically, that of multiple components woven together, underlapping and overlapping each other and so forming a connected unity that, while difficult to disentangle, still manifestly comprehends distinct elements.

As for *war,* authors of books like this one are accused from time to time of exploiting terms from more physical fields of human

---

[5] *Webster's Third New International Dictionary* (Springfield, Mass.: G. & C. Merriam Company, 1961).

endeavor to impart a specious drama to their prose, which would otherwise be all too prosaic. To defend myself against such attacks (!), I observe that the word *war* seems ironically to be derived[6] from Old High German *werran*, "to confuse," which suggests that its first use in a military context must have been not at all dramatic, but instead somewhat sedative.

In any event, *war* scarcely needs to be defined here. *The war on complexity*, by contrast, can usefully be glossed. By this phrase I mean:

- Simplification of business practices
- Global standardization of business practices
- Centralization of systems
- Automation of *all* lines of business
- Progressive movement toward self-service
- Acceptance of management by fact
- Deployment of suites, not kits, of business software
- Reduction or elimination of modifications to vendor software

To state a simple truth, business is—and always will be—a complex endeavor. This truth is illustrated by the fact that e-business software must relate every one of the eight bullet points above to every other one. The purpose of business software is not really to eliminate complexity, but rather to concentrate it as much as possible within the software domain, thus freeing humans of prolonged, tedious, and mind-numbing responsibilities. So it might be more just to speak not of *attacking* complexity but of *corralling* it. On review, we see that the first of these six bullet points relate to simplifying and clarifying *human* experience; only the last two directly address the simplification of software.

The wonderful thing about simplification in business is that it initiates a virtuous circle. Simplifying a business procedure makes that procedure easier for employees, partners, suppliers, and customers to understand—and to practice. They will use it more often, and in doing so they will generate more business data, which serve as the raw material for expanded business intelligence, which in turn enables not

---

[6]Ibid.

only strategic decisions but the further simplification of business practices. This cycle recalls Blake's concept of human experience as helical, with the soul progressing iteratively through phases that repeat themselves, yet experiencing each phase at a level higher than before.

Here are other examples of how this cycle works:

Simple and intuitive interfaces reduce training costs, freeing time and funds for further initiatives in simplification. They also encourage self-service, freeing administrative time and costs to be used for similar initiatives; also, by conferring ownership of data on those who are responsible for the data, they promote data accuracy; this advances business intelligence, and so on.

Global deployment of one set of business processes is indistinguishable from standardization of those processes. Its effect is to train a user in Tasmania to deal with an application and an interface that he encounters while he is stationed in Tajikistan. Again, superfluous training costs are eliminated. Global deployment also implies a degree of round-the-clock support, which argues in favor of self-service.

The elegance of such cycles is usually obvious. For instance, a business suite that produces meaningful business intelligence could be used to view not only the number of leads coming in every day, but also the channels through which those leads came, the campaigns or press releases associated with them, and the sales groups to which they were assigned. Suddenly sound decisions could be made much more quickly than before, by virtue of rapid access to all the relevant facts. It would become far easier to understand how to deploy marketing dollars.

Simplification of Business Practices

When a business application is modified to accommodate a complex business practice, the expense of the modification is only the first in what may prove to be a long sequence as the application undergoes repeated upgrades and integrations. When the business process can instead be simplified to match the application (Fig. 2-1), the investment will usually yield immediate and ongoing returns.

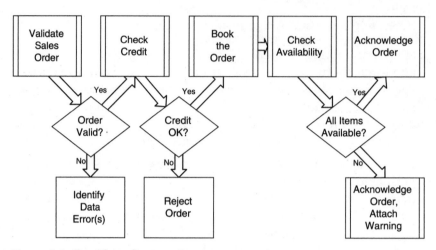

Figure 2-1. Simplifying Business Practices

As an example of a business process that may or may not be complex, take entitlement enforcement. When somebody calls a company for support on its product, how does the company verify who the caller is and what rights he or she has? Clearly it is sensible for the company to maintain, at most, a single record identifying the caller—not one per national subsidiary, not one per line of business, not one per corporate language, not one per data center, not one per company the caller is associated with, but one per caller. If the call is placed on behalf of Company XYZ, the company being called needs a single global record identifying Company XYZ; that record may link to multiple records, each defining a single contract, but the point is to keep the data structures as *simple* as they can reasonably be and as *few* as they can be.

Big companies have traditionally fragmented their data; indeed, they have generally had to do so. Now that the Internet has made it possible to concentrate all business data, it has at last become clear how expensive it is to maintain—and to try to depend on—multiple scattered records that nominally represent a single entity, whether that entity is a customer, employee, or business partner. Transferring customer data across telephony networks, call centers, and Web systems to ascertain and enforce entitlements—or for any other reason—is a business practice that can, and *must*, be simplified.

As a rule, any business practice that the CEO doesn't understand, or can't understand at once, is too complex. It would be constructive for CEOs to take such understanding as their prime criterion, because the importance of the drive for simplicity merits the continual attention of somebody with the power to get the job done. It makes sense for debate to be encouraged, for issues to be resolved promptly, and for key decisions to be taken at high corporate levels, not delegated.

Global Standardization of Business Practices

The argument *against* global standardization of business practices (as represented by Fig. 2-2) was that corporate subsidiaries in distinct nations found it difficult or impossible to communicate with each other in detail. This was the extenuation for the use in different parts of the globe of business practices that were traditional in their ambient cultures, or of practices that regional executives preferred for more idiosyncratic reasons. *They*, after all, were the ones who were effectively running their subsidiaries, and it made a lot of sense to allow them to run them as they pleased.

The advent of the World Wide Web made short work of that argument, leaving nothing to oppose the flood of arguments *in favor of* global standardization. We have already noted that such standardization makes it easy for Employee E to do his or her job effectively from any point on the earth's surface. More important, it means that the top executive officers can easily understand what's happening in Europe and compare it to what's happening in North America or in East Asia; their advanced understanding gives them the ability and the authority to enforce *their* writ around the world. But this can be true only when accounting practices in France are reconciled with those in the United States, when sales cycles in Germany are defined the same way they are in Australia, when the contract renewal process is identical in China and in Peru.

This is not to deny that localizations of some kinds are useful, indeed indispensable. Invoice numbers serialized autonomously,

Consolidate Your Business Information
Better Information, Lower Cost

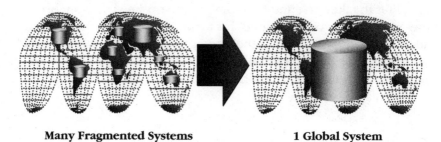

Many Fragmented Systems   **1 Global System**

Figure 2-2. Global System Consolidation

communications in local languages: these are easy to justify. But the use of standard practices wherever reasonable increases the visibility of the global business from the corporate head office, making it easier for the company to formulate and to promote an integrated and appropriate business strategy.

Centralize Complexity, Distribute Service

A major theme in the evolution of computing has been the centralization of complexity and control. Consider some of the professionally managed networks with which we deal every day:

- Gasoline
- Radio
- Telephone
- Television
- Water
- Utilities
  - Electricity
  - Gas
  - Sewerage

Although each of these systems involves great complexity, we nevertheless take them for granted. Why? Because, to the highest reasonable degree, that complexity has been distanced from the consumer. To be sure, automobile engines and television sets remain complex devices, but—with allowances for their effective functioning—they have been simplified and commodified to a very high degree, and the most important result has been their ever-increasing reliability and ease of use.

Consider television. The concept underlying television technology can be stated in a few words, but the technology itself is fantastically elaborate. And, beyond the technology, television as a social construct incorporates recording and live broadcast studios, programming and scheduling, negotiations and contracts for intellectual property rights, advertising campaigns with ad splicing based on viewer demographics, and standards for transmission (sometimes including encryption); satellites, cable, land lines, and towers enabling transmission; and complex billing systems involving a majority of viewers. What contribution is required from the viewer? To press a single button; to pay one monthly fee. Why can't the service provided by software be just as simple?

As the computer network matures, it will follow (fast!) the tracks laid down by older networks. Microsoft likes to tout Windows 2000 as the most complex engineering project ever undertaken by man. And so it may be: a Manhattan Project for our time. But who wants the atomic bomb—or any other product of monstrous complexity and dubious stability—sitting underneath his or her desk?? Imagine an *electric* system that could not improve your service without your purchasing a $500 upgrade—a system that might crash time and time again and, to be debugged, might require a highly trained technician to visit your basement!

From such a system, in which your PC is trapped, the Internet offers emancipation. In effect, the home PC will become simply one more appliance, connecting to the Internet as your taps connect to the municipal water system, your radio to the airwaves, your phone to the telephone network, your refrigerator to the electric grid.

Compare surfing the Web to channel surfing. Again, the technology underlying the experience is of awesome complexity. And, beyond the technology, every Web site is the end result of content creation and development, sometimes very extensive; it also relies on a production environment and may be supported by staging and testing servers, performance labs, and databases scaling into the gigabytes. Then the connection of the viewer to the site relies on complex networks, traffic patterns, and routing over multiple Internet routers, with the networks themselves being owned by multiple partners. Again there are elaborate standards for transmission and complex billing arrangements, and now we find centralized ad servers for personalized content. Yet, again, the only requirement of the viewer is normally a few clicks—sometimes only one—of the mouse. On the occasions when the viewer must type in an entire URL, we recognize this as the price of having an effectively unlimited set of destinations—a feature that television has yet to offer us.

The Internet makes possible the establishment of global standards for a corporation's business practices. Likewise it makes possible the centralization of IT systems. No longer is there any need or justification for maintaining an IT staff and system in each country where the corporation does business. Centralization enables enormous savings on IT equipment—and on staff, which can be redirected to functions that are not redundant.

The key to success is to centralize complexity and distribute service.

Automation of All Lines of Business

Companies often set the bar for automation too low, emerging with systems that automate some processes or business areas but leave others untouched by inhuman hands (so to speak). Fissures between areas of automation can be terrible impediments to business flows. Imagine trying to automate a lead management process with no telemarketing system, an exchange without procurement, customer care without contracting, a sales process with no Web store and no self-service quoting and approval system. Every gap will complicate the relevant processes and enlarge the costs of processing; margin improvements that might have been expected from partial automation will be threatened or annulled by too-frequent transits across the human/machine interface, which will obstruct data flow and compromise the data.

If a business is to be automated in part, it makes sense that automation should be provided to support complete business flows in one area of processing, then expanded to cover other areas according to the same principle. But the greatest benefits are incurred when all areas are automated using software that can communicate effectively from every area to every other. Two applications that are isolated from each other can never generate as much useful business intelligence as two that interact, and this principle gains strength as the number of applications grows. Thus the ideal is comprehensive and pervasive automation of the enterprise's business practices, something that any company can achieve by using a comprehensive e-business suite (Fig. 2-3).

I acknowledge that most businesses are not ready to throw out their current applications to make room for an integrated suite. This concern is addressed in Chap. 3 under the heading "Heterogeneous Implementations." More general observations about how companies can move forward along the path I'm describing appear in Chapter 8.

A Comprehensive E-Business Suite

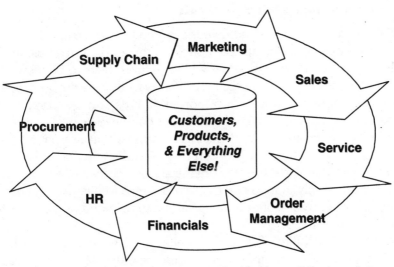

Figure 2-3. Comprehensive Automation as Enabled by an E-Business Suite

Progressive Movement toward Self-Service

Any enterprise that has a global system has an incentive at least to accommodate (if not to conduct) business constantly. Some such enterprises will need to staff for 168-hour-per-week support, but many will not, assuming that they provide self-service functionality for their stakeholder community—their customers, employees, business partners, and members of their demand and supply chains.

This is the first respect in which self-service can displace serious business expenses. The second respect consists of the fact that not all work that must be done need be done by company staff (except when the process is employee self-service); instead, it may be done, willingly, by somebody else. The third respect derives from putting a degree of data control in the hands of those who are most knowledgeable about the data and who bear most responsibility for them. (Needless to say, all other data need to be kept private or given read-only status.)

Yahoo! and Amazon are outstanding examples of continuous conduct of worldwide business based almost entirely on self-service. A business cannot scale effectively without standardizing on self-service systems for customers, employees, partners, and suppliers.

Acceptance of Management by Fact

Software suites for electronic business can collect and marshal data, to a large extent automatically, subject those data to business intelligence systems, and generate well-organized facts to be viewed (via self-service) by senior executives. Sales forecasts can be based directly on input from sales reps; order figures can be compiled directly from customer orders; the status of contract renewals can be updated by the customers and business partners that are parties to the contracts. Marketing budgets can be based directly on leads and assigned, with the leads, to sales organizations. Partner effectiveness can be automatically graded and displayed. Employee counts, quality measures, and a myriad of other data can be maintained or generated and displayed at need.

The sheer availability of crucial business data, which can now be much more timely, comprehensive, and standardized than was possible even 10 years ago, means that executives will depend much more heavily on business facts. Interpretations will vary, but the ability to cast any set of facts in various lights by using sophisticated business-intelligence programs will also make it easier to test and revise any interpretation. Strategic executive decisions will come to be based much more firmly on objective foundations, and force of personality will diminish rapidly as a determinant. The days of fist-pounding executives who simply "know" the business truths and will not brook fact-based dissent are numbered—and the number is small.

Deployment of Suites, not Kits, of Business Software

With this subject and the next, we proceed to simplification not only of business processes and practices but of the software required to support them. In doing so, we must concede at the outset that the primary purpose of such software is not to be simple. Relative simplicity, to be sure, is a hallmark of elegant software. But even so, business software must logically be at least as complex as the processes it supports—and should be more so, because it can cost-effectively add functionality (as for business intelligence) that goes beyond what humans could reasonably do without the software to support them.

To argue that business software must be complex is not, however, to argue that such complexity is a virtue, or that it ought to be multiplied. In fact, the shortcomings of needless complexity are obvious to the imagination, even if you can't see them on the display facing you. When programs from multiple vendors are hooked together, each will often retain its own graphical user interface (GUI), meaning that users of such a system must accustom themselves to various design conventions, to buttons with similar names but different functions, to differing display elements (calendars, for instance), and so on. More serious for the business using disparate products are discrepancies in the database schemas, which must somehow be coordinated but can seldom be fully reconciled, whatever the outlay.

Possibly this problem can never be fully solved. The most comprehensive suite of business software will never perform every possible business function, and as additional functions are developed, or judged worthy of inclusion, the result will involve some retrofitting, with the usual compromises and inefficiencies. Even so, the problem can be minimized; the way to do so is clearly to design as much functionality as possible from the ground up—or, more literally, from the database up. Discrepancies and disparities at the user level, though they may sometimes horrify prospective purchasers, are easy to recognize and often easy to correct; meanwhile, grotesque inefficiencies are often tolerated at the database level because they are "transparent to the user."

Every company that follows the kit ("best of breed") approach in developing its system runs the risk that it will select a unique combination of products, thus presenting the system-implementation effort with an unprecedented challenge. Proven methods of integration often will be commercially unavailable even for relatively common sets of applications. Some vendors whose offerings do not cover the full spectrum often must coordinate with a familiar third party, which might be (for instance) SAP for back-office applications; in such cases they occasionally develop and then market a standard integration method. This is, of course, a material service to prospects that want to implement the designated combination of programs; even so, it typically means building APIs to interface between two distinct database schemas, so that the result requires more storage than is logically necessary and operates more slowly than analogous combinations of programs that are designed from the start to share a single schema.

In short, purchasers of business suites may indeed find that they must—for a while—do without the functionality that some "best of breed" choices would have provided; but they will be compensated with other advantages, including

- Reduced storage requirements
- Reduced processing times
- Reduced implementation costs
- Reduced implementation times
- Reduced training requirements
- Increased control of business data
- Increased ability to exploit advanced features of system components
- Progressively increased compatibility with other customers' systems as standards emerge for basic business functionality

Reduction or Elimination of Modifications to Vendor Software

Modify vendor software? Why?

Do we modify our automobiles? Well, those of us who enjoy such work certainly do; and people who enjoy modifying vendor software should be encouraged to continue, though perhaps they should be charged for the privilege.

What most of us do with our cars is to select a standard design and then choose among a set of standard options. Think for a moment about what this has meant for the evolution of the automobile: every brand has been able to incorporate every major advance in design, because the factories have not been busy reworking every unit to the purchaser's preconceptions about how (e.g.) the transmission should work. But the convention with software has been for companies to purchase standard products and then pay somebody to change those products so that they conform to the company's peculiar business processes. And who is that somebody? Either an employee, who is probably familiar with the company's business processes but not with the software product, or a consultant, who is probably familiar with the software product but not with the company's business processes.

In a more rational world, the peculiarities of rival sets of business processes would gradually be ironed out, as I suggested previously, with the consequence that vendors could concentrate on evolutionary advances in software and their customers could communicate and coordinate with one another much more effectively. Such an evolution is not consistent with the expenditure of huge sums to make sure that each new generation of software does things in the "XYZ Corp. Way."

Modifications to vendor software are typically slow and expensive. Even those that cost-effectively achieve the desired effects carry penalties that may prove crippling to the customer. Modifications typically invalidate any warranties offered by the vendor; they create serious difficulties for the customer in trying to upgrade to later releases of the modified software; and they may introduce conflicts with other products from the vendor that the customer later needs to implement. This in turn robs the customer of the ability to implement swiftly the software that can execute on management's latest change of strategy.

Whatever the scope of the applications offered by a given vendor, the vendor's responsibility is to ensure that those applications discharge in a logical and cost-effective way every conventional business function that falls within their scope. With their e-business suites, a few vendors have set out to do just this. Such suites cannot pretend to do everything that every customer may want, whether or not in the way the customer wants things done. Instead, they are designed to fulfill the functions that are essential to the conduct of 21st-century business; and, because they are so designed, their vendors typically want customers to use those suites as delivered.

Only a broad standardization of the essential business practices can put a stop to the needless complexity of customized systems, with their huge costs of ownership, functional fragility, shortfalls of scalability and upgradability, and heavy burdens of support. Vendors need to bring finished, comprehensive products to market; customers need to learn to use those products in the form in which they leave the vendors' hands. The potential rewards are mind-boggling.

Wallet Share

Prospective purchasers of business software naturally care deeply about what the software is going to do for their companies. They also need to care deeply—and, as a rule, they do—about the total cost of ownership (TCO) of that software. TCO merely *begins* with the cost of the software license, which usually is greatly exceeded by the other expenses attendant on getting new software up and running—and keeping it running and up to date. These include the costs of:

- Business process reengineering
- Customization
- Integration
- Training
- Support, maintenance, and upgrades

What do these costs amount to? According to a report from AMR Research,[7] "Only 24% of the cost of CRM is represented by the applications; users should plan for at least a three to four times

---

[7]"Report Card on CRM," AMR Research, February 2001.

multiple for infrastructure and services." AMR presents a table of CRM budget guidelines by size of company:

	Company Size		
Benchmarks	$5 Billion	$1 Billion	$250 Million
Hardware/networking	$ 4,786,273	$1,017,453	$ 210,596
Applications	$ 5,542,000	$1,228,300	$ 269.360
Software technology	$ 5,038,182	$1,100,341	$ 232,890
Services	$ 6,297,727	$1,021,079	$ 188,952
Headcount	$ 4,534,364	$ 813,341	$ 180,403
Total CRM budget	$26,198,545	$5,180,515	$1,082,202

Further guidance comes from Lou Gerstner, CEO of IBM, who told analysts[8] that "for every dollar spent on the application . . . there's . . . three to seven dollars [spent] on services." Notably, Gerstner appears to be neglecting some of the costs obviously associated with implementing, maintaining, and upgrading software.

Evidence[9] from more than a thousand software implementations indicates that companies spend some $8 to $12 on CRM implementation and maintenance for every dollar they spend on CRM license fees. (See Fig. 2-4.) This ratio, which is the effect of today's parts-and-labor approach to system implementations, is often difficult to justify in terms of the benefits conferred by the software implemented, and recent articles in the high-tech press report increasing customer impatience with the difficult and protracted process of putting newly acquired software to practical use.

Such considerations will drive the increasing displacement of kit solutions by e-business suites, marking the evolution of the software industry from a parts-and-labor model to a finished-goods model. Suites as implemented may be expected to enable rapid response as effectively as kits, if not more so; but their relative ease of implementation will itself exemplify rapid response—and, by doing so, will shorten the path to responsive corporate systems. I expect that, within five years, suites will have cut the implement-and-maintain ratio to $3.50-$4.50 per dollar of license fee, as shown in Fig. 2-4. By

[8]On IBM Analyst Day, May 2000.
[9]Originating with McKinsey & Company.

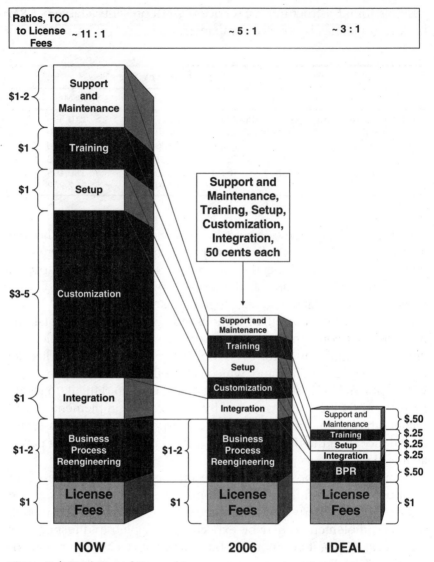

Figure 2-4. Total Cost of Ownership

far the biggest reduction, I anticipate, will be in the area of customization; ideally, the costs of customization will disappear, together with the practice thereof.

Nevertheless, the enormous savings to be achieved by such an improvement will not by any means exhaust what is theoretically

Savings to be Achieved, Ideal Case (Assumes License Fees Constant at $1)

Area	Current Costs	Ideal Costs	Reduction
Business process reengineering	$1–2	$0.50	50 to 75%
Integration	$1	$0.25	75%
Customization	$3—5	$0	100%
Setup	$1	$0.25	75%
Training	$1	$0.25	75%
Support and maintenance	$1–2	$0.50	50 to 75%

possible. World industry can gain benefits as yet almost unimaginable by moving on toward more homogeneous business processes supported by more homogeneous software. Such progress, no matter how great, can never eliminate all expenses associated with the adoption of new software, but it can continue to reduce them and may indeed drive customization costs close to zero, as suggested in Fig. 2-4. My view is that an implement-and-maintain ratio of $2 or less per dollar of license fee is ultimately achievable. Competition among software vendors, as among software users, is going to move the world in this direction.

Summary

To repeat, attacking complexity means:

- Simplification of business practices
- Global standardization of business practices
- Centralization of systems
- Automation of *all* lines of business
- Progressive movement toward self-service
- Acceptance of management by fact
- Deployment of suites, not kits, of business software
- Reduction or elimination of modifications to vendor software

These themes are all interrelated. Centralization is essential to globalization. Globalization will force standardization and simplification. The automation of all lines of business will promote system use, thus making possible the collection and analysis of more data, which will allow enhancement of the system—leading to greater use, more data, and further improvements. The system will increasingly produce *facts*, which can serve to replace the assumptions and hyperbole on which executive decisions have too often been based.

This whole process can scale effectively only through the implementation of self-service, which will promote further system use by customers, employees, partners, and suppliers; this increased involvement will drive further iterations of the data/process improvement loop. And this organized attack on complexity is the goal of suites of business software that can be implemented out of the box. Suite users can expand and improve their businesses by leveraging the work of thousands of software engineers—over and over again, release by release. To do so cost-effectively, they must refrain to the maximum from changing the software released—from "breaking the seal."

The war on complexity *can* be won. Winning means taking complexity off the shoulders of the company's stakeholders and corralling it within a single global instance of the business software.

3

The E-Business Suite

Introduction

The past five years have seen a profound upheaval in the commercial landscape. Businesses all over the world have been working feverishly to transform themselves into e-businesses, convinced that their ability to compete depends on their doing so. They are not mistaken.

What are they trying to change? What is an e-business?

An e-business is distinguished by the deployment of its data, which must meet several exacting standards:

- Its data and business rules reside in a single integrated database.
- The database is customer-centric.
- The database can be accessed globally via the Internet.
- Data access is mediated by easy-to-use applications that require little or no training.
- Ideally, those applications are tightly integrated—and by design, not by afterthought.

Moreover, an e-business has consolidated and centralized its computer operations.

The Internet is the key to this model. Before the Internet, every global enterprise relied on multiple databases as a necessary evil—necessary, because Tokyo could not depend on data in Chicago; evil,

45

because multiple databases meant duplication of data, conflicting data, inconsistent data formats, and potential multiplication of effort whenever information needed updating. Evil, moreover, because multiple databases meant multiple data centers and multiple information technology (IT) staffs.

With the Internet, multiple databases remain an evil, for all the same reasons; but they are no longer a necessity. Every company leading the e-transformation must be moving toward one central database of purged, reconciled, and integrated business data, maintained by one IT staff in a single data center. This process will be iterative and evolutionary.

Some businesses have been down this road before, creating and populating giant data warehouses that turned out to be gigantic wastes of effort. Yes, it's true: data consolidation can be botched! And it's a risk to get out of bed in the morning, but you won't achieve much by staying in it. Readers may estimate for themselves what business structures can be built successfully on foundations of unreliable and inconsistent data.

The business benefits that e-business suites confer on their users are potentially enormous. Customer employees, anywhere on the globe, can use consistent and intuitive interfaces to access business data that are more reliable than ever before. Data integration will enable business intelligence that is more subtle and comprehensive than has ever been possible. Companies can execute to a single product and price book, to a single contracts system, and to a single master record per customer. Executives, newly able to exert control that is both tighter and more responsive to dynamic business needs, will come to manage less by rhetoric and more by reality. Centralized databases will enable fully integrated e-business flows that span all major corporate applications: marketing, sales, service, e-commerce, contracts, interaction centers, business intelligence, and so on.

And that's not all. Corporate expenses for training, for IT staff, and for computer equipment will plummet. Most important of all, system implementation will become simple, speedy, and straightforward, and companies will save the sums that they would otherwise have to spend—and have spent in the past—on gigantic system-integration projects.

It is crucial that any e-business suite be both complete and integrated. (By *complete* we mean that every customer relationship management (CRM) or enterprise resource planning (ERP) application needed—marketing, sales, service, contracts, buy- and sell-side e-commerce, financials, manufacturing, collaboration, accounts payable and receivable, general ledger, human resources, etc.—is included in the suite. By *integrated* we mean that every application in the suite has been engineered around a unified global customer and product database. (See Fig. 3-1.) All the applications must have been designed and built by the vendor to work together

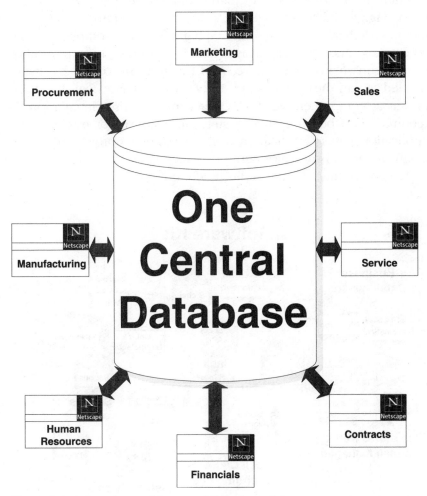

Figure 3-1. A Complete and Integrated E-Business Suite

and share information. So no systems integration is required to install such a suite.

In contrast, some vendors' CRM offerings require systems integration—a lot of custom programming and a lot of architectural reconstruction—to make the different applications in the suite work together. That's because none of those vendors designed and built most of the applications it offers; instead, they filled out their offerings by partnering with or acquiring other companies. So what? Why would anyone care?

When the various pieces of many competitive offerings have not been engineered to fit together, a systems integrator has to glue them together. That systems integration is complex, time-consuming, and very expensive. In fact, systems integration labor usually runs many times the cost of the software or the hardware needed to run the system—and the customer has to pay for it. To install a comprehensive CRM suite, no systems integration is required. And because such a suite must consist of true Internet applications, every application works in every country, every major language, and every major currency.

One contrasting offering is illustrated in Fig. 3-2.

Figure 3-2. A Kit Based on Acquisitions and Alliances

Global Operation, Complexity Worsens

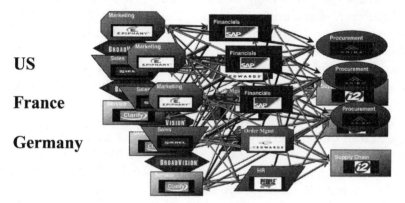

US

France

Germany

Figure 3-3. The Kit Approach Extended Beyond National Borders.

The set of offerings illustrated in Fig. 3-2 derives from a strategy of product acquisition and product resale. The result is a product set that is not complete, not integrated, and not global; hence it is a kit, not a suite. It is very difficult and expensive to install. Once it is installed, the customer has multiple systems with multiple customer and product databases. The data fragmentation caused by the multiple databases makes it more difficult to get needed data out of the system. For most business flows, extracting business intelligence is impossible.

This picture gets worse. The kit approach, pursued by multiple vendors, can—and often does—expand to contaminate all of a customer's lines of business (Fig. 3-3). What a mess!

Trick or Treat: Hershey's Halloween

A discouraging example of what can happen when a company adopts the "best of breed" approach is provided by Hershey Foods.[1] In mid-July of 1999, Hershey implemented a $112-million computer system relying on software purchased from Manugistics, Siebel, and SAP, and integrated by IBM consultants. The company then lost control of its distribution system just in time to fumble Halloween, the biggest candy

[1]Hershey's troubles were discussed in articles in the *Wall Street Journal* Interactive Edition for Oct. 29, 1999 and in *Computerworld* for Feb. 2, 2000.

date of the year. Despite having plenty of candy on hand, Hershey could not distribute it reliably to its customers, who turned to rival manufacturers to shore up their supplies; Hershey salespeople took to calling customers much more often than usual in order to find out whether shipments had actually arrived. Hershey's profits were down 19 percent for the third quarter and 11 percent for the fourth; wholesale customers were especially unhappy, because they were often being blamed by *their* customers for Hershey's problems.

An up-to-date CRM suite keeps all your customer and product information in one place—a global CRM database. Your employees know where to look to get the up-to-date information they need to service your customers. And your customers can use the Internet—7 days a week and 24 hours a day—to access key sales and service information. Your service levels go up—while your service costs go down. Your sales go up, while the cost of sales goes down. And your business scales.

The Kit Trap

Remember the days before the Internet? Suppose that an American multinational had built or assembled a computer system that it considered ideally suited to its business environment. Naturally enough, executives at corporate headquarters would have encouraged the top executives in Germany and France and Japan and Britain to use the same system. Or perhaps not *exactly* the same system: they probably would have understood that the system would be modified in each country to suit that country's business environment. But even if they didn't understand that this was going to happen, it was inevitable that it *would* happen.

And why not, after all? Until the late 1960s, when EDI (electronic data interchange) was developed, systems in different countries could communicate with each other—in volume—only by shipping tapes and disks back and forth. Though EDI made it somewhat easier to exchange data across national borders, it was still complex and expensive; so, for most companies, it remained more important for the system in France to suit the French business climate than for it to communicate readily with the system in England.

Some multinationals, of course, used a system in the United States that had been built in the United States and a system in France that had been built in France. But even when two systems began as twins, they would start to diverge when used in different countries. And this was generally not a problem.

Until the rise of the Internet. At last, and suddenly, it became easy to exchange data between systems halfway around the world from each other. And so it became easy to see how difficult it was for alien systems to communicate.

The average multinational now found itself presiding over a network of loosely interconnected systems, each with its own private language, that had to learn almost from scratch how to communicate with one another. Multinationals had fallen into the kit trap: the use of diverse systems that are difficult to reconcile because they were designed and developed without reference to any need for complex interaction. Suddenly global access was easy: employees, customers, and business partners could access the corporate systems from almost anywhere on the face of the earth. But global access to a globalized system was still only a dream.

By definition, software kits are antithetical to rapid response. Corporations have business data that they need to keep centralized, tightly organized, and reconciled; software kits scatter and disperse those data, often maintaining them for one application or one country in a form that makes them meaningless to another application or another country. Reconciling the forms in which the data are maintained often solves only a part of the problem, because each application or national system often still insists on maintaining its own copy; this multiplies data-maintenance problems and costs, and it leads without fail to inconsistencies among the multiplied records.

The complexities associated with maintaining a distinct system in each country of operation are costly and dangerous. Overlaying them, through successive upgrades, with the complexities associated with multiple distinct versions of the software is a recipe for business suicide.

Do the job once. Do it globally.

The Meaning of E

What is the beginning of the end, the end of the infinite, and the beginning of eternity?

Answer: the letter *e*.

As everybody knows, *e* is the most frequent letter in English . . . and its use has not declined with the rise of the World Wide Web, which has produced "e-" versions of almost everything. Even before the Web, the letter was hard at work in the acronym *ERP*, which stands for *enterprise resource planning.*

My thesis is that, within the context of software applications for business, *E* for *Enterprise* has been largely crowded out by *e* for *electronic.* For a few years, this second *e* generated wild enthusiasm and excitement not only among software professionals but also among investors and even the public at large; then, ever since April of 2000, it has increasingly been recognized as the first letter of exaggeration, excess, embarrassment, and extinction, in approximately that order.

But *e* is going to stage a comeback. Without losing the meaning *electronic*, it will gradually take on the connotation *efficient.* The two words are *not* synonyms, and efficiency will often dictate the use of more traditional media, which will continue to be vital elements of business activity. Complete business flows will include face-to-face encounters and paper trails as well as call centers, Web transactions, and the like—both within the enterprise and across the extraprise. *E* for *efficiency* must increasingly characterize all channels and all responsibilities in the business organization—all lines of business and all stakeholders. As it does so, electronic channels will increasingly be perceived as the most cost-effective for almost every activity that can exploit them. As the forest of e-companies continues to thin out, it will become easier to recognize that more traditional companies *must* turn decisively to electronic business if they wish to survive.

Efficiency is at the heart of the argument for business suites and against business kits, and the conduit for suite efficiency is the complete business flow. To appreciate this point, compare the Internet store you can implement using BroadVision products to any comprehensive solution for employee and business self-service sales. With BroadVision you get the ability to capture an order over the Internet—but not the ability to fill that order, nor to feed it to your accounting or available-to-promise (ATP) systems or to any other sales process or customer-care application. What, then, do you do when a business customer abandons a shopping cart, or when a purchase needs special approval?

With a comprehensive suite, an order passes through to the financial applications in real time; it interfaces with configuration, marketing, promotions, pricing (and specialized price lists), and ATP as needed. Order and payment statuses are definite and can be viewed at all times. The sales process is integrated across many applications, including those for telesales, field sales, and partner sales. Employees can generate quotes and can forward these to internal administrators, for approval, or directly to customers. Customer care agents can step in to help businesses and employees complete and place their orders; most of the business-to-business (B2B) orders are placed in accordance with outstanding contracts.

To accomplish the same level of business coordination with BroadVision, customers would need kits consisting of products from Clarify, E.piphany, Siebel, Kana, and the like, not to mention vendors of ERP applications; these kits would need to be glued together by IBM or some other systems integrator, and they would come without instructions. With true demand chain automation, the Web store is a feature of the product, not the only product of a niche vendor.

Some History

The market for business applications, now 50 years old, has a rich and complex history. Though it can be divided into many phases and developments, these tend to overlap extensively; some are "merely" history, while others help to define the current environment and still others are mostly in the future.

ERP

The applications that fall under this heading lent themselves more obviously to automation in the decades before the 1990s; they were also perceived as having more direct impact on the corporate bottom line. The result is that the market is more firmly established and more mature than that for CRM. It has experienced four generations of contestants.

The first generation included a lot of highly specialized vendors— some of them marketing systems for accounts payable but not accounts receivable, others vice versa. This degree of nonintegration, now almost unimaginable, was effectively overcome by a single company, McCormick and Dodge. M&D's ERP product was designed for mainframes; it never made the transition to client/server configurations, and today it is forgotten. M&D was bought by Dun & Bradstreet in the late 1980s, then merged with MSA (Management Science America) as D&B Software; that, in turn, was sold to Geac Computer Corp. in 1996.

ERP has a big functional footprint, covering financials, manufacturing, human resources (HR), order management, and purchasing. In consequence, the second generation saw an explosion of ERP vendors. The advent of client/server computing led to a profusion of development tools and a multitude of affordable solutions; companies of every size could find serviceable products. The vendor population grew to exceed 100, the leaders being Baan, J.D. Edwards, MSA, Oracle, PeopleSoft, Ross Systems, SAP, and Walker Interactive.

The third generation witnessed the start of major attrition in the ERP market. Companies that survived the shakeout were those that offered a broad suite of ERP applications (Oracle, SAP), those that specialized in one area (as did PeopleSoft in HR), and those that aimed at a specific range of customers (JDE, small-to-medium enterprises). Together with Baan, these four were the major competitors left standing.

The fourth generation arrived in 1999. Baan proved unable to make the shift from client/server to the Internet; after nine consecutive quarters of major losses, it was acquired in mid-2000 by Invensys plc, as a part of which it has revived a bit, though permanently diminished. Ariba, Commerce One, and i2 emerged as vendors of software for the procurement and supply-chain markets. PeopleSoft, though late to the Internet party, eventually emerged with a reasonably comprehensive suite of ERP and CRM products. It joins Oracle and SAP as one of the strongest players in the ERP space.

CRM

CRM, to which automation came later, is now entering its third generation. The first generation consisted principally of Software Artistry; Astea, a vendor of automation for customer care and field service; and Brock International (now Firstwave Technologies), which sold automation for marketing and sales. Each company was a leader in its field, executed a high-profile IPO, and—for a while—maintained a high market capitalization.

Each, however, failed to react promptly to the demands of the CRM market. Customers were looking for one or more vendors that could span sales and service applications; they also wanted vendors that addressed multiple channels of customer interaction, particularly call centers and mobile applications. Software Artistry was acquired by Tivoli Systems, which was acquired in turn by IBM; IBM scuttled Software Artistry one year later. Astea and Brock both peaked in early 1996.

These plunges marked the start of the second CRM generation, which proved to be dominated by sales and service vendors. (Vendors of marketing automation, although they did appear, did not come into their own until later.) The four firms that were dominant in this period were Clarify, Scopus, Siebel, and Vantive; a late arrival on the scene was Oracle. The four leaders shared a strategic vision, foreseeing an integration of sales and service functionality for mobile professionals and for call-center operations. But each took its own path: Clarify focused on service and on vertical markets, Scopus on customer care and call centers, Siebel on sales, and Vantive on service and mobile applications. (Remedy also emerged, but principally as a vendor of automation for internal help desks; in 2001 it was acquired by Peregrine Systems.)

The 1998–1999 period saw the end of the second generation, with several of the leaders being swallowed by larger enterprises. Clarify was acquired by Nortel, Scopus by Siebel, and Vantive by PeopleSoft. Meanwhile, the landscape was transformed by a general recognition of the centrality of the Internet. By designing its CRM suite for the Internet from the start, Oracle managed to capitalize on its late entry; Siebel seems to be making a successful transition from the client/server universe. A whole new class of vendors has emerged, including Agillion, BroadVision, E.piphany, Kana, and Silknet. The market space is also being invaded by a number of nontraditional participants offering point solutions; the most important of these is Cisco, with its acquisitions of GeoTel, a vendor for call-center middleware and routing applications; of WebLine, an e-mail-interaction-management vendor; and of Selsius, an IP-telephony vendor.

An Internet arena of particular interest is e-commerce. Players in this space include Oracle, Siebel, and PeopleSoft, but press coverage has focused on two relative newcomers, Ariba and Commerce One. Both companies supply software for the implementation of online exchanges, but their business models differ: Ariba's revenues depend principally on license sales, whereas Commerce One aims to generate revenue mostly from exchange transaction fees. While Ariba's early lead in mindshare has dissipated, the stock price of each company has declined so far that both appear to be candidates for acquisition.

Another company of importance in this context is i2, which is older than Ariba or Commerce One and has established itself as a leader in software for automating supply-chain interactions; this is clearly a mission of greater complexity than merely enabling one-to-one deals. i2 aims to help its customers to reduce inventories and cost of goods sold and to accelerate product times to market.

The dominant medium is now the Internet; the dominant applications continue to be for marketing, sales, and service; the dominant targets are call centers and mobile agents. And the dominant vendors are Siebel and Oracle. Going forward, the victorious vendors will be those that can develop integrated suites that address as broad a range as possible of CRM targets and applications.

Customers, Transactions, and Obligations

Every company has customers, transactions . . . and obligations that link the two together. What can we say about these in relation to the kit-versus-suite dichotomy?

Customers

As relates to customers, the essential distinction between the kit and the suite approaches is that the e-business suite provides you with a single global customer master record. This will not be done by any kit, as assembled. Any kit that reaches this goal is a kit that has had several of its components modified so that they no longer use the database schemas they were designed for.

The single customer master record will become the focal point for all lines of business and all domains: marketing, sales, service, contracts, financials, procurement, and buy- and sell-side e-commerce.

It will promote the ability to understand installed-base information and profitability. It will ease new product introductions and transaction flows, and it will enable sales reps to up-sell and cross-sell. And it will slash the cost of information . . . in contrast to the kit-based equivalent, which results from a consulting-led integration of incomplete data sources and structures.

Transactions

Here the analog to the global customer master record is the unified global product catalog. Such a catalog arms the enterprise to respond rapidly: users can quickly add, change, or delete records for products, bundles, prices, and promotions; these changes take effect globally, across all lines of business and all systems areas—Internet store, quoting systems, partners, telesales, financials, marketing, direct sales, and so on. Large-scale changes can be made over a weekend.

Again, the problem with the kit approach is that it brings with it a multiplicity of database schemas. Many, if not all, of the kit components will arrive each with its own product tables, and users will have to accept the inefficiencies of maintaining multiple sets of product data—or those of reworking the kit components so that they all look to a single product catalog in the corporate database.

Obligations

Transactions are sticky things. Each has an associated contract (or obligation) that binds it to the customer, as to the vendor. The span of contracts is broad, as shown in Fig. 3-4.

In the world of software kits, corporate systems and divisions have splintered views of every sales order. Order Management has an incomplete sales order agreement; Procurement has the terms of purchase; Financials has the terms of payment; Service has stand-alone warranties and renewals. Pricing agreements are confined to people's heads, and sales personnel fall back on "Let's make a deal." The result is to disadvantage both parties to the contract. How can the vendor competently up-sell to its customers? How can it update contractual terms to be applied to new contracts of all types? How can purchasers arrange for consistent levels of service?

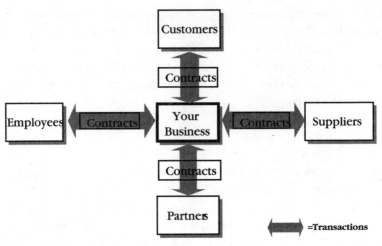

Figure 3-4. Contracts

For . . .	Items
Buying	Procurement agreements
Making	Project plans
Managing	Master agreements
Monitoring	Service-level agreements
Selling	Sales orders, sales-based contracts
Service	Warranties, entitlements
Use	Intellectual-property rights, leases

While there has long been a need for contract management software, a number of "pain points" intensify the need:

- Contracts have become more complex and more numerous.
- Lax contract management leads to lost revenue.
- Rising customer service expectations require more active contract management.
- Tighter regulatory compliance necessitates closer contract oversight.
- Improved contract management can yield impressive ROI gains.

Contract management software can address all these problems by automating and standardizing contracts, making the information in them visible and measurable. Such functionality is essential to e-business suites because contractual agreements pervade the operations of every business (Fig. 3-4).

An e-business suite with a sound contracting component enables the use of master agreements with prenegotiated standard terms and conditions; it allows the application of business rules across contracts of all types. Sales reps can place quotes and orders for customers on the basis of master contracts, and can account accurately for those quotes and orders. Customers have the ability to place orders off of such contracts, initiating the flow of those orders through the vendor's internal systems. The vendor's Internet store is reliably linked to the vendor's business partners, sales reps, and order administrators. As a result, clerical staff can be greatly reduced, and order-management centers turn into facilities for expectation handling.

Software as a Service

Many businesses do not have the resources required to implement a full e-business suite, while others prefer to outsource the work to be done. They are accommodated by the trend whereby packaged software is gradually giving way to services. In the context of this book, this trend can be understood as a relatively quick and easy way for a company to immerse itself in an e-business suite environment.

For customers, the reasons for this trend are manifold:

- Many top executives have no IT experience. Many of these are somewhat mistrustful of their company's IT efforts and suspicious of the large budgets often allocated to those efforts. Desiring greater control over the full breadth of their enterprises, they form a natural constituency for services that can be presented as relatively standardized and available at more predictable rates.

- Services can typically be implemented, if not immediately, still much more rapidly than licensed software. They allow ROI to be realized and measured much earlier.

- Services allow up-front investments in hardware and software to be effectively eliminated.

- Services accommodate much-reduced investments in preparatory planning and training.

- Costs of development are reduced or eliminated.

- Maintenance and upgrade responsibilities are off-loaded. Conflicts and other issues relating to versions disappear, because there is always *only* the current version. New features become available more promptly and reliably.

How much customers have to gain by escaping from the traditional cycle of development, implementation, maintenance, and upgrade becomes clear when we scrutinize that cycle:

1. Gather requirements.
2. Produce a Marketing Requirements Document.
3. Produce a functional specification.
4. Ensure the availability of a large and complex hardware infrastructure.
5. Produce a detailed design.
6. Produce a detailed project plan, identifying scope, resources, and schedule.
7. Write the software.
8. Write the setup procedures and administrative functions.
9. Port the software, as appropriate, across x hardware platforms and y operating systems.
10. Package the software for distributed installation.
11. Manufacture the CDs, print the documentation, stock the warehouses, ship the product.
12. Stand by for—or assist in—hundreds, perhaps thousands, or (with luck) even millions of installations.
13. Translate the software and the documentation.
14. Return to step 1.
15. Endure long, complex, and various upgrade cycles.

Passing through the first 13 steps of this model has typically taken software companies as long as two years. But two years is a geological epoch; it is *not* an Internet development cycle, which is a period so brief that it dictates a development framework accommodating real-time software enhancements. This means enhancements in minutes, hours, days, weeks—perhaps, at the outside, in months. In short, e-business means the decline of packaged software and the irresistible ascent of online services.

Software vendors also have many reasons to promote the trend toward services:

- Services will tend to make their revenue streams smoother and more predictable.

- Overall costs of software support will presumably decrease, enabling vendors to market more cost-effectively to small and mid-size businesses.

- Revenues from new customers can be realized more promptly.

- Delivery costs will be reduced, often almost to zero.

- Maintenance and customer support will be facilitated by increased centralization and control. The increased scope of service responsibility will potentially be more than offset by compensatory revenue.

This convergence of the interests of software sellers and software buyers will increasingly cut into traditional software licensing. I expect that, by 2006, 50 percent of software use will be via services, and that by 2011, 80 percent will be.

Services come in two distinct flavors, somewhat confusingly termed "online services" and "application services." Together with the traditional arrangement for software, they constitute three current models (Fig. 3-5).

The ability to upgrade one's online services as rapidly, and as often, as is required by the needs of the company or the pressure of competition—this presupposes a framework underlying the application that is flexible and skillfully designed. It is not an unusual experience to visit a site for eBay, eToys, E*TRADE, Netscape, or Yahoo! and to find that the user interface has changed dramatically. Likewise, you may visit Amazon.com and see that the site offers a new product line or a major new service. And when have you needed the training manual for E*TRADE or Amazon to complete your errand?

SOFTWARE MODEL:	ONLINE SERVICE	APPLICATION SERVICE PROVIDER	TRADITIONAL
HARDWARE/ SOFTWARE LOCATION	*IMMATERIAL*	*AT ASP SITE*	*AT CUSTOMER SITE*
SHARED DATABASE?	*YES (WITH VPDs)*	*NO*	*NO*
MAINTENANCE	*NOT APPLICABLE*	*ASP*	*CUSTOMER OR OUTSOURCED*
ACCESS	*INTERNET*	*INTERNET OR VPN*	*CUSTOMER LAN*

Figure 3-5. How Software Models Compare

This is a services model, and it comes with a new set of rules and methods. Software companies, under pressure from their customers and competitors, will gradually evolve in this direction.

Examples of online services that are emerging to displace packaged applications are

- Account and contact management
- Customer care
- General ledger
- Payroll
- Spreadsheets
- Storefronts
- Surveys
- Word processing

Examples of sites that provide robust, scalable, and reliable online services are

- eTravel.com
- FormulaOne.com
- NetLedger.com
- My.Oracle.com

In a Down Economy
Business Trade-Offs

As we noted earlier, the four measures of corporate success are market share, revenue, cash flow, and profitability. Every company's senior executives need to assess each of these and to steer the company toward the desired combination. They need rapid response, made possible by software that supports such assessments, that enables sensitive adjustments to the course they are steering, and that generates prompt and reliable feedback as to the effects of each adjustment. Little time must be lost between their business decisions and the implementation of those decisions in the corporate systems.

In any economy, an e-business suite can be a cost-cutting engine. In favorable economic environments, the suite can be a platform for growth; in unfavorable ones, it can be a lifeline. During economic upturns, needed skills are difficult to find; hard decisions can be deferred, redundancies tolerated, and low-hanging fruit left to be plucked another day. Mistaken IT decisions can be filed under "continuous improvement." During downturns, a single wrong IT decision can put you out of business.

Getting Married

. . . that's what you're doing with your e-business suite vendor. You're not doing lunch, having a date, courting, or getting engaged. You're making a serious commitment—for richer, for poorer, in sick economies and in healthy ones.

Over the last 14 months, the business-software sector has seen enormous attrition and consolidation, with many IT vendors driven out of business—and it's not over yet. Your commitment to an e-business suite means betting your company's future: getting married means a major long-term commitment.

Making the Tough Decisions

In up economies, businesses can afford to defer difficult decisions. Suppose you select ten application providers to automate all your business needs: you haven't made a major commitment to any one provider, and you haven't had to decide where automation is most urgently needed. No trade-off has been necessary.

Matters are different in a down economy. Now it's crucial to identify the low-hanging fruit: the opportunities for automation that promise the greatest return for the least effort and investment. Now it's imperative to focus on inefficient business practices and those that won't scale. Battle will be joined daily. The company's top executives must step up to the tough decisions; they must make the trade-offs and become agents of change.

Heterogeneous Implementations

All major companies—indeed almost all companies—are already using software products, and most are likely to hesitate before replacing even one of their current applications. For most such companies, throwing out all or most of their current systems in order to standardize on a single e-business suite is simply not an option. One reason is that stand-alone or kit applications will in some cases offer features that a suite may not match, or that they conform more closely to the company's way of doing business—if only, perhaps, because they're helping to get that business done. There's no reason, in fact, why some applications from other vendors cannot coexist over the long term with an e-business suite, or most of a suite. (Figure 3-6 suggests how disparate elements can be bound together within a single integrated system.) It's only that every such application that remains in use will mean ongoing integration, maintenance, and upgrade expenses that the company using it might otherwise avoid.

Consequently, vendors of e-business suites have a responsibility to their customers and prospects, and to themselves, to provide migration paths to their suites that accommodate many small steps and do not require one giant leap. For most vendors, this means that they need to construct their applications so that they interface (without unreasonable effort) with customers' existing information architectures, and vice versa. For IBM, Microsoft, and Oracle (and

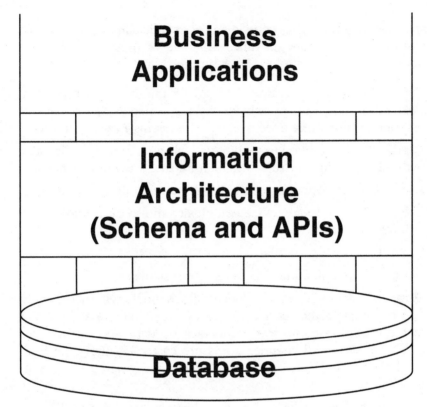

Figure 3-6. Abstract E-Business Software Configuration

other database vendors), this compatibility requirement extends to the database as well.

Every e-business suite vendor will presumably encourage its customers to move toward a configuration in which its suite is fully exploited, even where some competitive applications continue in use. But vendors need to understand that presenting suite prospects with an all-or-nothing choice is going to result in a lot of sales of nothing. During transitions, some of which will prove to be perpetual, vendors need to stand ready to support heterogeneous implementations and to provide maintenance for heterogeneous configurations.

Nine Steps for a Down Economy

Even so, there are steps that any company can take that will minimize the need for trade-offs—steps that can improve cash flow, market share, profitability, and revenue in any economic climate, but that are vitally important in difficult times. All nine of these steps will be supported by any comprehensive e-business suite.

1. Choose a business solution that can be implemented for a low price in a fixed time. Not only do executives need systems that will respond rapidly, they need to get such systems *in place* rapidly.

2. Put the chosen solution to work iteratively and incrementally. Start with the low-hanging fruit—the high-impact, low-effort initiatives.

3. Focus on your core competencies—do *not* modify software.

4. Use the solution to centralize complexity and to distribute service and information.

5. Expand markets: go global.

6. Do so by implementing a global single instance.

7. Move to low-cost channels. Electronic channels will increasingly be perceived as the most cost-effective for almost every activity that can exploit them. But companies need to apply consistent standards across all channels to assure customers the same high level of service regardless of how, when, and where they initiate contact.

8. Move to self-service. By slashing administrative time and costs, implementation of self-service methods works to minimize the harm done when staff must be cut. Also, by conferring ownership of data on those who are responsible for those data, it promotes data accuracy; this advances business intelligence, which forms the foundation for improved business processes.

9. Manage by fact.

Step 1: Low Price, Fixed Time

In a thriving economy, any successful company may develop a "tomorrow the world" attitude. Ironically, this can mean a reduced sense of urgency when it comes to implementing complex global applications, and the process may drag out for 18 months or longer.

In a stumbling economy, the same attitude can lead to damaging layoffs, to loss of markets, and ultimately to corporate failure. Low-price, fixed-time software implementations, which ought to be standard in all economic environments, become essential when revenues, staff, and other resources are constrained.

Step 2: Low Effort, High Impact

Ideally, e-business suites will be designed and developed in such a way that each can be implemented either incrementally or all at once. The big-bang approach that might be selected in an environment of rapid growth may be less appropriate in harder times, for which an incremental and iterative approach is well suited.

All businesses have process inefficiencies. As a rule, it makes perfect sense to look for the processes that can be rationalized and optimized with the least effort and expense relative to their potential contributions to the bottom line. Business processes that are often promising candidates for reform include

- Opportunity to forecast
- Problem report to resolution
- Contract to renewal
- Quote to order
- Procurement to payment

Your first e-business application is the starting plank in an information platform. As you add applications, that platform grows broader, sturdier, and more serviceable. Every plank helps to support those next to it, and the construction that results is essential for the support of any up-to-date business.

Step 3: Focus on Core Competencies

Expect the vendor of your e-business applications to act as the software expert. Let the vendor change and extend the software, if necessary—don't do it *for* the vendor. In short, focus on your business; don't be a computer hobbyist.

Modifying vendor software is far more expensive than it may seem. Not only does it add to the cost and defer the first benefits of your system, but it means additional costs as far as the eye can see, because *you* become the owner of the modified software. Finally, your changes to the software get in the way of later vendor upgrades and thus compromise your ability to profit from ongoing development on the part of the vendor.

Step 4: Centralize Complexity, Distribute Service

A major theme in the evolution of computing has been the centralization of complexity and control. This process underlies the expansion of distribution systems for gasoline, radio, telephones, television, water, and utilities—each of which is easy for the public to consume in the amount desired.

Although each of these systems involves great complexity, we nevertheless take it for granted. Why? Because, to the highest reasonable degree, the complexity has been distanced from the user.

Consolidating your customer data and your IT operations can enable improved service and operations at the same time that it generates enormous savings.

Step 5: Expand Markets

Expand your reach among customers, partners, and suppliers at a time when failing businesses are leaving *their* trading communities looking for safer harbors, and when cutbacks by your competitors are lowering *their* levels of customer service.

The most sweeping way to expand your presence is to set up one or more Internet storefronts and exchanges, enabling global buy-side and sell-side e-commerce. These can serve to enable transactions with your suppliers and other business partners; they are almost indispensable for firms that can deal directly with consumers of their products and services.

Step 6: Global Single Instance

Consolidate and simplify your software systems to the fullest extent consistent with the functionality your business needs. Put all your data for customers, for products, for everything, in one place; then let your stakeholder community access it, as you authorize, over the

Battling Complexity

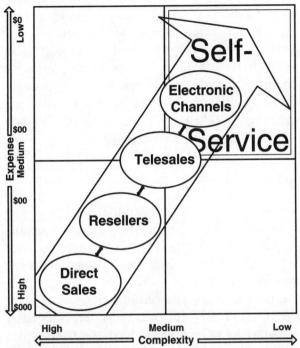

Figure 3-7. Attacking Complexity Means Cutting Expenses

Internet. To move toward self-service is to move toward reduced expenses and complexity (Fig. 3-7).

The more databases you maintain, the more your data are fragmented, and the less information you can derive from the data. Consolidating and reconciling your business data is the single biggest step toward institutionalizing savings.

Reduce the number of vendors and the volumes of integration code.

Trade off what you merely want for what you urgently need.

Reduce hardware, labor, redundancy, and rework.

Slash internal dependencies among lines of business and operations in countries abroad.

Step 7: Low-Cost Channels

The number of channels over which businesses can conduct transactions is continuing to grow. Once, all business was face-to-face. Now it can mean interaction by phone, through TV, by e-mail, by chat, or by real-time communication across the Internet.

The challenge for e-businesses is to provide high and consistent levels of service across all channels while driving interaction as much as reasonable to the channels that prove most cost-effective. Face-to-face interactions, such as those provided by direct sales forces, are typically the most expensive. Call-center operations are less so, and Web-based interactions are usually the least expensive.

Step 8: Self-Service

Any enterprise that doesn't implement self-service functionality is wasting money, time, and labor. Self-service systems enable customers, employees, partners, and suppliers to conduct their own transactions, displacing administrative efforts that can amount to 30 percent of prior expenses.

Promoting wider participation in your applications ecosystem means that transaction volumes rise and data-entry errors decline. The result is greater volumes of more reliable business data, which can lead directly to improvements in business processes and to sounder executive decisions.

Step 9: Manage by Fact

Use corporate systems to assemble, interpret, and present the facts effectively, generating the business intelligence needed to support the decision-making process.

The Destination

Where will these steps lead?

> *To improved margins.* Companies will be able to recognize great savings in internal costs by using comprehensive e-business suites.
>
> *To more effective management.* Top executives will gain corporate insight that will be more detailed, more timely, and more fact-

based than ever before. They will learn to found their decisions increasingly on factual information and less on their feelings about where their companies may be going.

To improved business practices. Simplifying a business procedure makes it easier for employees, partners, suppliers, and customers to understand—and to practice. They will use it more often, and in doing so will generate more business data, which serve as the raw material for expanded business intelligence, which in turn enables not only strategic decisions but the further simplification of business practices. The cycle reinforces itself and continues.

AND the Winner Is . . .

Taking these steps will bring any business to an information architecture that makes sense for its customers, its employees, its partners, and its suppliers. That architecture will enable the business to scale as needed when the time is right, and it will provide the support the business requires in order to hold steady through times of economic challenge.

Summary

The NASDAQ Composite Index does not define the business climate for high-tech companies and their customers and business partners, but it has a lot to do with it.

Figure 3-8 shows every swing of 10 percent or more in the index over the last five years. Apart from the fantastic anomaly of the dot-com boom, the most conspicuous development reflected is the enormous increase in volatility over the last 18 months.

To profit from the heightened volatility of business conditions, every company needs to arm itself with systems that not only enable rapid and flexible response but can sustain the bottom line in downturns and fuel expansion in upturns. A respectable e-business suite should enable the companies that use it to differentiate themselves in all business conditions. The suite must be comprehensive, to meet the requirements of large and midsize firms. It must accommodate implementation in stages, thus allowing for system growth at a pace that accommodates the needs and abilities of its users; in so doing, it will meet the requirements of small companies as well. Regardless of business conditions and regardless of company size, the e-business suite is likely to prove a strategic and cost-effective solution.

NASDAQ Composite Swings > 10%

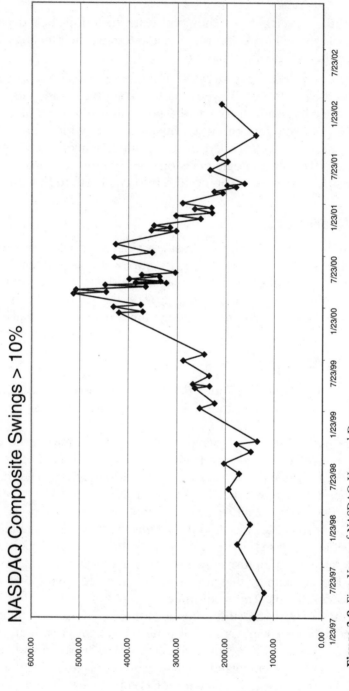

Figure 3-8. Five Years of NASDAQ Ups and Downs

4

Entering Global Markets

Introduction

The challenges of doing business abroad have always been daunting. Early obstacles such as warring competitors, hazardous seas and geography, catastrophic weather, and new lands inhabited entirely by hostile foreigners have been largely overcome; companies now face the similarly challenging problems of having to reconcile business practices involving multiple languages, currencies, and tax structures, subject to local and international laws, while taking into account varying national and regional customs, all within constantly shifting political climates. As I write, there are 191 nations, with diverse laws governing contracting, financial accounting, labor, and manufacturing practices; there are perhaps 300 languages of commercial importance, and at least 100 currencies that merit consideration.

A company that is doing a successful domestic business might take one look at these challenges and decline them. Some will decline them by default, without ever taking a serious look. And sometimes such decisions will be sound. But any company for which international business has serious promise needs to make its decision with care, mainly because the decisions it takes today as to systems architecture can keep open its windows on the rest of the world or can close them for good. And the same is true for decisions it fails to take.

The decision by any multinational to begin doing business in nation N will have an impact on many of its areas of business:

- Marketing will have to accommodate N's Robinson list of people that have asked that their names be excluded from marketing efforts through e-mail and other channels.

- Sales forecasting will have to be done in N's currency, even though it may later be converted to another currency for rollup.

- Service, in many cases, will need to maintain defect information specific to N.

- Contracts will require invoice serialization specific to N.

- Finance will have to wrestle with N's tax code and perhaps with national regulations and conventions related to closing the corporate books.

- Manufacturing will need to address the movement of goods within N.

- Procurement will need to abide by N's laws and conventions relating to payment.

- Human Resources will need to respect N's labor laws.

Yet it has never been easier for a business to go global, and to do so while increasing its efficiency, taking greater control of its business, and expanding into additional countries—becoming a rapid response enterprise. Advances in three areas have made this possible: the Internet, technology standards, and integrated, globalized business software.

Whether it is making the transition from a local business to a global one, seeking to expand a global presence, or consolidating global operations, any business that hopes to succeed in the world arena faces multiple tasks and challenges. Its executives need to consider the following points:

- Significant decisions regarding the company's business practices, systems, and persona will be required.

- For mission-critical activities, the company will have to move from a workweek of five days, eight hours per day, to one of seven days, twenty-four hours per day, by leveraging global labor and "lights out" IT.

- Business processes will need to be automated, and outward-facing processes will need to be automated first.

Nevertheless, it must be obvious that no company will make its business less complex simply by going global. With regard to business complexity, the great virtue of resolving to go global is that it presents the company with an unprecedented opportunity—an opportunity that will be squandered, unfortunately, if company executives treat expansion into foreign markets as merely a technical initiative to be delegated to the IT staff. Instead, global expansion needs to reflect a deep strategic resolve to identify long-range corporate goals and to standardize on global business processes—before stepping across the border. When approached in this spirit, the globalization of the business can prove a strong ally in the war on complexity.

Decisions, Decisions, Decisions

All the world's a stage, but any company hoping for a long run needs to make some decisions. Specifically, it must assess its business practices, programs, and persona to see how they play to a global audience.

Are You Ready for Global Operations?

It is all too easy to erect an Internet superstructure on top of current business practices, to implement current practices on the Web without paying attention to the underlying business logic. Business processes may not scale to global dimensions, but inefficiencies in those processes often do. Any company that is migrating onto the Internet and joining the global marketplace needs to assess its ways of doing business and to rethink its business logic in the light of the new global economy.

Which business practices need to be considered? All those involved in buying, selling, and fulfillment, as well as in customer care and support.

Which business processes meet the requirements of global operations? How must the others change? To understand the milestones on the road from traditional business to electronic business, companies must ask and answer essential questions regarding their present business practices—questions concerning business processes and the tools that support them. These questions address the following areas:

- Sales
- Lead management
- Orders
- Inventory
- Marketing
- Contracts
- Financials
- Product catalog
- Customer records
- Regional considerations

For each area, I've outlined some questions. Read them as a chief executive might, and note which issues might be critical for your business. Also consider which business processes could be better supported by your tools, and which of your tools can do more for you than they're doing now.

Sales

Can you review opportunity data and identify which opportunities your sales organizations are committing to?

Can you see multiple views of that information—one by manager and one by salesperson?

What is your up-to-the-minute global sales forecast? This is a simple question, but it is tough to answer. A global sales forecast must cover your revenues from licenses, product renewals, support contracts, Web-based sales, call center telebusiness, direct business, mail catalogs, and business through partners and other channels. It must extend to your customers, opportunities, and pipeline. It will consist of at least three numbers: one for the best case, one for the worst, and one for the most likely. Forecasting needs to be simple and flexible, and it needs to reflect managerial judgment all the way up and down the chain. Some will forecast thoughtfully, examining their pipelines, win probabilities, close dates, sales processes, and competitive information. Others will forecast by plugging in a number: "I will do $X this quarter." Forecasts may be based on opportunity data so detailed that one could rely on them in quoting a price and placing an order. At the other end of the spectrum, they may be based on product-category summaries ("X units of Y"). In all cases, every manager needs to forecast in the local currency, and all forecasts must be rolled up globally, using applicable conversion rates, to a single reporting currency. And the forecasting system must run on the Internet, on handheld and wireless devices, on laptops, and on cellular phones—all through self-service, with no training required.

Sales forecast intelligence is even more critical than at first it appears, because sales staff are often misled by native enthusiasm into feeding improbably optimistic projections to upper management. Typically there are at least two views of every situation—management's view and that of the sales force. Reliable sales intelligence is thus essential if management is to marshal and prioritize resources in such a way as to optimize sales performance.

Stages in the progress of potential sales can and must be distinguished reliably, and the progress of each sale needs to be closely tracked. Especially after some historical statistics have been accumulated, this method will enable much more accurate projections than most companies can currently generate. Here are the stages that count:

1. Lead
2. Callback
3. Opportunity (qualified lead)
4. Proposal sent
5. Collateral sent
6. Quote issued
7. Demo given
8. Reference issued
9. Undergoing our approval process
10. Undergoing customer approval process
11. Won
12. Lost

Thorough business-intelligence measures will address every stage in the sales process, culminating with the final and most important stage, the won/lost distinction. The executive whose sales team is predicting a billion dollars in sales this quarter, and whose own forecast is even higher, needs to sit up and take notice when only a few weeks are left until the end of the quarter and quotes have been issued for only $400 million worth of prospective sales.

Lead Management

Do you know how many leads came into your business today? This is another simple question; but complexity soon enters. How do your leads group by geography, by product, by line of business? Leads come in via e-mail and bingo cards; they come in via direct responses and from installed-base details and third-party lists; they come from partners, events, seminars, your Web site, press releases, field sales, field service organizations, and abandoned shopping carts. You need also to know what press releases have been issued, and to what audience(s). Were these tied back to your Web site, enabling the collection of prospect information that may mature into actual leads?

Leads need to be graded and then assigned to available employees with appropriate skills. Some go to business partners; some sit idle for a time. They mature, and are assigned—and assigned a sales credit. Some leads turn into opportunities; some die.

Now imagine this happening in 60 countries and in 10 languages. What happens when organizations fight over leads, contesting territorial authority?

Suppose your business issues a press release introducing a new product and directing readers to your Web site for additional information. Suppose you are also running a new TV commercial, sending out e-mail proposals, and initiating a new call-center campaign. Can you measure the cost-effectiveness of each initiative in terms of leads generated?

Orders

What orders are in and booked, right now?

Can you follow an order as it matures to an opportunity, to part of a global sales forecast, and finally to confirmation? What determines whether business is booked or closed—sales, shipping, order administration, revenue recognition?

Do you know how many orders are generated through your Web site, through your interaction center(s), through your partners, through your retail sites?

Do you know how much business has been quoted, how much quoted but not signed, how much signed but not booked, and how much booked but not processed because of some constraint, like a shortage of materials?

A comprehensive e-business system will include functionality for tracking orders and fulfillments. It will need to track orders across their full life cycle, showing orders entered, value booked, value shipped, value invoiced, revenue recognized, and cash received. It should also monitor exceptions and risks specific to this business process-represented by unbooked orders, shipping backlog, unearned revenue, and open receivables.

Inventory

Can you quickly determine what products exist, in which locations, in what configurations, and in what condition, for sale or service?

Suppose a needed repair part is available in multiple locations. Can you determine which is the least expensive part and path to meet the needs of the job?

A full understanding of the global inventory position is the foundation of a rapid response to an available-to-promise inquiry. Increased visibility of more and more links in the supply chain will enable your e-business to carry a much leaner inventory and to cut expenses associated with it. Will your current inventory practices scale to a global level?

Marketing

Can you state your exact global (or even local) marketing expenditure, and identify what proportion of that expenditure converts to booked orders?

Can you measure the success of any campaign by region, by product, by channel?

Can you identify what leads and opportunities have been generated and what interaction channels were most used by consumers?

There are many valid objectives for marketing campaigns: to create awareness, to create demand for products or for training, to generate leads, to promote the electronic sales process. Ideally, you can measure the effectiveness of a campaign according to any or all such criteria—and then tweak or terminate the campaign as appropriate.

Contracts

Does your contracts process support global visibility and analysis across all managed contracts?

Do you have standard definitions of terms and conditions, including payment terms, sales credits, price lists, deliverables, and assigned tasks? This standardization facilitates the deployment of best practices.

Can you create new contracts easily, taking advantage of standard text stored in a common area?

Can you track a contract's progress through its life cycle and define the operations that are currently valid for each contract? For example, *active* status for contracts of certain types may mean that they can be updated only via change request; in certain cases, *hold* status may disallow service entitlement.

Are you automatically notified when contracts are up for renewal, and can the renewals be handled automatically?

Which contracts must be renewed this quarter? Which have quotes outstanding, which have been invoiced, and which are booked? Which are encumbered with incomplete or incorrect customer data? How long does it take to renew the average contract, and how much staff effort is involved? Can you map your potential workload to contract terms and the available labor pool? What is your goal for service renewals—70 percent, 80 percent, 90 percent, 95 percent, 99 percent? Do you want to merge and co-terminate contracts? Will you make or lose money by doing so? Can you up-sell levels of service? And which are your most important customers as measured by contractual commitments?

Many businesses will have multiple contracts with each of many customers. For example, Oracle Corporation has 10 or more contracts with more than 20,000 businesses, 30 or more with more than a thousand, and 100 or more with some 500.

Financials

These are discussed later in this chapter under the heading "Some Financial Issues."

Product Catalog

Can you quickly add, change, and delete product specifications, configurations, prices, and promotions?

Can you implement such changes to products and services in all countries, all major currencies, and all lines of business simultaneously and quickly—over a weekend, for example?

Once implemented, such changes should be reflected immediately on your Internet store, exchange, and systems for direct and indirect sales, telesales and telemarketing, sales compensation, order management, accounting, and support.

Customer Records

Because of the way IT has developed, most large companies have multiple databases containing redundant customer data. The resulting complexity and inefficiency seriously counteract the advantages of global Internet business. To answer many of the questions posed in the preceding sections, you need a single source of truth for customer data. You want a customer record to be exactly the same whether it is viewed, for example, by sales staff using sales force automation (SFA) applications or by accounting staff using AR applications. The questions, then, are these: for each customer, can you reconcile the multiple records you may have into a single record that serves the needs of all internal users of the record? And can all your business applications use that record for their transactions? If either answer is no, then your software is not truly integrated.

Regional Considerations

Business practices will have specific variations that pertain to individual countries; a partial list includes taxation, pricing, delivery and return of goods, invoicing needs (such as serialization), contractual obligations, use of local languages and currencies, and human resource practices (relating, for instance, to hours of work and holidays).

Companies must also heed accounting regulations, government guidelines, and Robinson lists of people who have asked to be exempted from promotional campaigns.

Does Your Business Software Travel Well?

New processes and improved procedures need to be rolled out globally, simultaneously, with minimal system downtime. The time when the corporate operations in the United Kingdom (for instance) ran on a distinct system with distinct processes will soon come to seem like the Cretaceous Period. For any business dealing globally, worldwide simultaneous release is becoming the best and only way for software releases to serve all customers. No business with critical 24 × 7 activities can afford to shut down for upgrades, backups, inventory, etc.

Global business requires globalized software, which has a number of levels of sophistication. Though client/server computing is now dying, it compelled many providers of enterprise applications to learn and understand, for each country in which they did business, exactly what requirements had to be met. Globalized software can meet needs for multiple languages at the same time—for example, it can allow a French user to see an application in French and a German user to view the same application in German. But translatability means more than just displaying application screens and messages in different languages. The software must also be able to display screens in single-byte character sets (e.g., English, French), in multiple-byte character sets (e.g., Chinese, Arabic), and in different formats. Language differences extend beyond the look of the characters. Consider the differences between English and Arabic. English uses 26 letters, with capital and lowercase forms for each. The Arabic writing system uses 28 characters in cursive script, written right to left, with each letter having three forms depending on where it appears within a word—and a fourth if it appears by itself. There are no block letters and no upper- and lowercase. Global software accommodates such differences; a global application should display the same screen in either English or Arabic, depending on user preference.

Customer care and service begins with the face a company presents to its customers. The Internet attention span is short. Expecting customers to adapt to foreign systems will drive them to businesses that make no such demand. This principle extends also to employees: will staff at different sites be able to use business programs that support their native efficiency, or will they be forced to adapt to one-size-fits-none software?

Translation is just one aspect of globalization. Globalized business software must be able to handle varying address, phone, and date formats, including different calendars. Configuration parameters should allow on-screen forms to be adjusted for local laws. For example, blood type may be required on a human resources (HR) form in one country, while, in another country, privacy laws may prohibit such a request. Another key globalization feature is the ability to handle multiple currencies. Software will often support transactions in local currencies, but the currency used for reports should be selectable, and parameters used for currency conversion should be definable by the user.

Any transaction or requirement that business software cannot handle will have to be dealt with manually by employees—at greater costs in time and effort, and with additional opportunity for error.

How the Internet Sees You

A popular joke highlights one of the distinctive traits of the Internet. A dog browsing at a computer says to another dog, "On the Internet, nobody knows you're a dog."[1] The Internet gives a talking dog the ability to be judged on merit, not according to preconceptions. (And yes, the Internet has given brief life to companies with Web presences unmatched by their performance. But market adjustments inevitably came into play, and e-Darwinism has thinned the herd.) The point here is that, in becoming a global player, each company must decide how it wants to do business and how it wants to be perceived. This is a chance to define and refine the company identity as the company grows to the next level.

A Web presence that is created and administered at a single source makes it easy to have country-customized Web pages that maintain corporate consistency in terms of messages and processes. A single home page with a country-picker drop-down that leads to suitably translated and laid-out Web pages is the first step in establishing a global identity.

What are the most important countries to do business in? What are the key markets? Companies can achieve economies of scale by concentrating on markets associated with a few languages of exceptional global importance. Although a company may determine that each of its interaction centers is to support every language that is important in the region or regions the center serves, it will

---

[1]Peter Steiner cartoon, *The New Yorker*, July 5, 1993.

probably need to confine its official processes to far fewer languages. For example, although Oracle does business in some 60 countries around the world and produces versions of its products in 28 languages, it does its contractual business in only 8: Chinese, English, French, German, Italian, Japanese, Korean, and Spanish. Only in these languages does Oracle produce ads, budgeting, collateral, stores, Web sites, online services, and support. While some multinationals might want to add Dutch and/or Portuguese to this list, some such simplification is essential to meet the demands of "Internet time," to which e-businesses must march if new products and services are to be introduced at a competitive pace.

The End of 8 × 5

A global business must work 24 hours a day, 7 days a week. A company's trading community needs access to the company's systems for buying, selling, servicing, contracting, invoicing, and paying. Most of this access can be provided with automated systems available via a browser over the Web.

At the highest levels, for the Global 2000, deciding to go 24 × 7 means that both systems and employees must be available around the clock and around the calendar. People must be on the headsets, taking orders, providing support, moving product from warehouses, etc. For smaller companies, a 24 × 7 presence is still desirable, but it may consist of self-service systems that can automatically provide for many customer needs, backed up with rapid-response human communication where necessary. In either case, the software and hardware systems that support these activities must never sleep.

More Hours Can Mean Less Work

The Internet provides an important new ability for the operational aspects of a global business—the ability to simplify the IT environment even as IT requirements grow. This allows key decisions to be business decisions, not IT decisions. Global 24 × 7 systems availability does not mean tripling or quadrupling IT resources; it means centralizing and simplifying them. The goal is "lights-out" IT, a room full of servers at a single location, with proper backups, that can be left running, monitored by diagnostic software and supported by a small, highly skilled IT team—a system that can be thought of as an appliance, not a fragile, distributed life-support system. As we saw in Chap. 3, supporting a global operation on a single software instance is now possible. The Internet enables remote monitoring and diagnosis of problems. System maintenance and performance tuning can be accomplished by specialists at headquarters, perhaps thousands of miles away. Software systems can be installed and upgraded automatically and remotely.

No Time for Customized Software

High availability, the end of 8 × 5, presages the end of customized software and of armies of consultants conducting integration campaigns. This never-ending war is won by not fighting it any longer. Companies cannot afford to keep fighting it. Why not? Because customized applications need to be customized again whenever any application they depend on is customized or upgraded. Because, if software is customized, upgrades can no longer be easily applied; they become another project for consultants, leading to additional testing and debugging to make sure everything still works together. A key to high availability is simplifying. What could be simpler than not paying consultants to modify your software?

"Lights-On" People

For Global 2000 companies, people will also need to be working 24 × 7, and unfortunately there is no "lights-out" solution to this problem. Instead, think "lights always on!" Companies need to consider multiple sites spread around the globe such that whatever part of the world is in daylight is being served by on-duty staff. This would mean, for example, 8 × 7 shifts rolling from each to the next of three centers distributed around the world, thus covering the clock dial. Such centers might be located in San Francisco, Bombay, and London.

Outsourcing for Additional Staff

Providing 24 × 7 coverage can require both additional facilities and human resources and can represent a significant expense. A viable alternative to captive operations is outsourcing, now a $340-billion-a-year industry and growing at over 30 percent per year. Its focus is shifting from manufacturing toward intellectual functions like data entry and customer service, and toward even more specialized functions such as research and product design.

The work handled by interaction centers is a major area of outsourcing growth. Finance, accounting, and medical transcription services are other areas that lend themselves to outsourcing, and are finding takers. Savings of 40 percent or more are possible with outsourcing.

Although the processes that are outsourced have traditionally been peripheral to a company's core business, many companies remain reluctant to outsource, fearing loss of control and quality and thus of customer good will. Such fears seem to be unsubstantiated, however. Outsourcing providers, such as a number in India, are proving they can provide services that are not only faster and cheaper but also better. Part of the difference has to do with how the work is viewed. What an American considers a transition job, an Indian may consider a career position, and the Indian is likely to be better educated as well. Furthermore, to ensure high levels of performance for their clients, outsourcing providers place a strong emphasis on training (including training in client processes), an area that suffers in many domestic companies.

High Availability and Maintenance

Outward-facing systems need very high availability—close to 100 percent. As more functions become self-service, and as more and more transactions are moved to this "human-free" zone, it becomes apparent that these systems must be up and running even if back-office applications are down. For example, the order fulfillment system may be down, but the Web store continues to run. Order status and taxation features may not be available, but orders can still be taken; when the back-office systems come back up, customers can be sent e-mails giving tax, payment, and shipping information.

How do you reconcile high availability with the need for maintenance?

Before the advent of Internet software, most software maintenance got done on weekends and holidays. Typically, the workers responsible would take the computer system down at 5 P.M. Friday, or at 12 midnight or 5 P.M. Saturday. They would then work more or less frantically, installing upgrades, adding users or functionality, tuning performance, adding patches, and fixing bugs—sometimes beavering away until early Monday morning.

With the end of eight by five, however, there is no point at which service can be interrupted without risk of frustrating some would-be users. (As an example, Oracle has 1.2 million subscribers to oracle.com; replicating an updated database to a production server can take as long as 4 hours, during which time that server cannot support operations on that database.) So companies will have to decide, probably on the basis of usage records, which periods are least sensitive. Holidays are now less promising: when they fall within the workweek, they provide windows that are too brief to be of much use, and they are almost always specific to a single country. A fairly promising maintenance window begins at 5 P.M. Saturday, Honolulu time, and extends until 9 A.M. Monday in Auckland and Sydney; but this provides only 20 hours (18 when it's summer in Honolulu), compared to 40 hours if all that time fell (as "it used to") in a single location. Notably, even this period risks problems with Israel, where Sunday is a working day.

Furthermore, the maintenance stakes have risen sharply. I remember when one could apply a bad patch in the branch office of a bank and the tellers would shout, "Hey! It's not printing right!"; and then one could quickly back the patch out with no serious harm done. Such mistakes made in the workings of a global Web site could damage financial records for hundreds of thousands of customers before they could be corrected, and nobody would hear their shouts until it was too late.

This situation is further complicated by the new suites of integrated software. In the old days, each line of business (LOB) had its own programs and was typically insensitive to those for the other LOBs. Finance, HR, order management, marketing, sales, service: each depended on software that had little or no impact on the others, so that changes could be made in one area without risking operations in another. Now, not only do all lines of business reside in the same global instance, they compete for system resources: for disk space and for CPU cycles and memory. And they must serve, as appropriate, not only the company's customers but also its trading partners and its employees.

How, then, is maintenance to be done? Thoroughly conservative IT implementations would maintain a distinct disaster-recovery configuration that exactly duplicates the production environment (but is at a different physical location). Less conservative implementations, like Oracle's, might rely on the redundancy server for disaster recovery—a sensible if not ironclad approach, given that disk drives fail far more often than CPUs. In Oracle's implementation, every write to disk is performed simultaneously to two distinct disks; a production implementation that incorporated a disk redundancy server and was exactly duplicated by a disaster-recovery environment would perform every write simultaneously to four disks.

The normal IT shop for a major organization will also feature a staging environment that (again) exactly duplicates the production environment. This means, for many corporations, a capital outlay for hardware that at least triples the cost of the production implementation. This can mean very substantial expenses: at roughly $200,000 per server, the 18 servers required for staging, production, and disaster recovery would total $3.6 million. Testing, quality assurance, and performance tuning can typically be conducted on smaller machines or on the staging system, but in any case they do not need a configuration as complex as that required for the production environment.

However, the maintenance window that concerns us does not relate directly to the machines used for testing, quality assurance (QA), performance tuning, or disaster recovery; its necessary duration is simply the time required to propagate updated code and data from the staging to the production system.

What to Automate First

The Internet has revolutionized what is possible in terms of how business conducts global commerce—and, in many cases, what is possible has quickly become what is expected, as challenges are successfully met. The complexities of multinational operation have been met by the unifying, integrating, and simplifying forces of a new generation of automated business solutions.

What functions should be automated in going global (or even staying local)? All of them. But companies first need to automate their outward-facing processes. This is where visibility and impact are high and effort is low. Here, in a down economy, automation enables moving transactions to the lowest-cost channel; in an up economy, automation becomes a platform for growth. The outward-facing functions to automate over the Internet include

- Selling
- Buying
- Customer service

Global Selling

Never before has it been possible for customers to purchase goods and services with such ease, or for a company to reach a global audience with a single voice. A business partner can now access its leads and submit its royalty reports over the Net. Executives can manage their businesses across all channels and geographical boundaries. Field sales personnel, no matter where they are, can use simple Web browsers to access customer and deal information. The Internet is the backbone that makes all this possible.

Sales Force Automation

With Internet-enabled sales force automation (SFA) tools, information can be effectively shared across the enterprise and along the value chain to customers, suppliers, and partners. CEOs of multinationals can now view global pipelines and make enterprise-spanning forecasts.

Sales reps can use Web browsers to execute SFA software. This enables any company to run its business globally using one or a few installations, with a very low cost of ownership, and to access accurate and comprehensive business information in real time.

The selling process has benefited particularly in the areas of sales productivity, lead management, and decision making.

Online Stores

Global stores promise very impressive ROIs, to be achieved partly through automating and partly through standardizing the sales process. A comprehensive global store for a major corporation will deal in all that corporation's lines of business and all its products, all the currencies it recognizes and the tax implications of every purchase, and all the languages in which the corporation conducts business. It will serve all prospective buyers, and it will do all this from one central location—with order fulfillment handled, in most cases, from distributed sites.

A global store can serve not only the company's customers but also its employees, notably its order takers, direct sales agents, call-center agents, support-renewal agents, and a variety of clerical administrators. The company needs to ensure that all employees whose business responsibilities include price quoting and order entry have access to the store. This is because one of the store's most valuable functions is to enforce correct and uniform pricing, discounting, product configurations, and other terms from the electronic product catalog. Never before has there been so powerful a tool for ensuring that the same corporate persona is presented to all customers and prospects.

The global store should allow any user to choose among the currencies supported (perhaps for a quote on a product or configuration, not necessarily for an order) and among the languages supported. It needs to present a broad range (if not all) of the company's products, accommodating the possibility that some products are available only in certain configurations or in certain countries, and the possibility that prices may have similarly limited applicability. The store needs to be able to compute the tax consequences of any purchase, which in many instances means that its software must integrate with software from a third party that specializes in tax computation.

Global Buying

"You can see the computer age everywhere but in the productivity statistics," said Robert Solow, a Nobel prize winner in economics, speaking in 1987. The so-called productivity paradox was not unprecedented. Productivity did not increase significantly for nearly 40 years after the introduction of electricity, in part because it took that long for industrial machinery to be changed over fully to electricity. More relevantly to our discussion, it took that long for companies to change their business practices and redesign their factories to achieve the efficiency gains that electricity enabled.

We are again in such a period. The productivity gains enabled by the Internet have yet to be fully realized. For companies to secure those gains, they must do as they did for electricity: change the way they do business.

Corporate Buying Online

Buying online offers companies an immediate way to generate savings from the Internet. Direct purchases—as of components for manufactured end products—have been conducted electronically for some time, albeit not to a great extent on the Internet. Many items are made to specifications, contracted for with long-time vendors, ordered at different times by various groups or divisions within a company, with varying payment and delivery terms, etc. Such issues prevent corporate purchasing of this kind from changing quickly.

Indirect purchases, however—travel, building supplies, office supplies, employee software, computer equipment—represent potential savings in direct proportion to the size and geographic distribution of a company. Such purchases are often scattered across corporate sites and departments. Having independent relationships with hundreds of suppliers makes tracking total item use and negotiating volume discounts impossible. Are we using more mice? Or do mice multiply like coat hangers? Should we buy them individually, or have everyone order from themousethatroared.com?

With uncontrolled indirect buying, the penalty incurred is not just the cost of the items bought; it is also the cost of the transaction and the number of transactions. How many people need to approve the purchase of a mouse? A purchase that now costs $100 to process and involves several levels of approval can be handled via a Web-based application for less than $10, with no level of approval other than what is required by built-in rules.

Until centralization on a single instance was possible, you needed to be big enough to run a private corporate network to computerize and consolidate all your purchasing. Now you can negotiate with suppliers all over the world, list their items in your one corporate catalog, and insist that everyone use it. Not only can you negotiate better deals, you can know what you are saving on what, where, and how often. What has been scattered data becomes business intelligence. A mouse will not malfunction anywhere in your company without your knowing of it.

Exchanges

An exchange is a two-sided marketplace in which buyers and suppliers negotiate prices, usually with a bid-and-asked system, and in which prices move both up and down. Exchanges come in many flavors, but all or nearly all are procurement exchanges, although they often combine different types of buying and selling. For example, many exchange sites support auction activity but also support spot buying and provide catalog aggregation and other services as well.

A procurement exchange is a marketplace in which one or more companies offer goods or services for sale and one or more companies participate as purchasers of such goods and services. A company may figure on both sides in a procurement exchange. Procurement exchanges are playing an increasingly important role in supply chains, and the volume of this business is such that this category of exchanges will probably always be the most important.

Procurement is moving increasingly to electronic exchanges. The early Internet boom years saw a proliferation of independent exchange operators of all types. Revenue projections and the willingness of companies to suddenly change long-standing business practices were both inflated, and new breeds of exchanges came into prominence: industry consortia, exchanges run by industry players themselves, and private trading networks (private exchanges each involving a single sponsor company and its suppliers or customers). Once relationships are established on a public exchange, much of the activity then takes place on a private network, thus ensuring the privacy of sensitive information that many companies are unwilling to present openly for all to see.

Exchanges exist for all major categories of business, and some exchanges serve more than one: aerospace and defense, automotive, aviation, life sciences, metals, construction, energy, food, human resources, paper, retail goods, technology, telephony, rubber, and transport, to name some but not all.

bal Customer Service—the Endless Summer

nt service is a powerful customer motivator; increasingly, it is service, not products, that provides competitive differentiation. Doing business on Internet time—24 × 7—means taking care of customers 24 × 7. By staffing three regions around the globe, companies can provide "follow the sun" service and support. While this may sound like a major effort, it need not be. A true e-business uses the full power of the Internet to make its operations more efficient. Advances in information technologies, combined with the access offered by the Internet, mean that the ability to support customers can grow more quickly than the cost. The Internet enables resources to be leveraged in ways that were just not possible before.

Service agents can be armed with complete customer information, so they no longer need to transfer customers or put them on hold. Even information that would traditionally be stored in a separate system is available. For example, if a customer has a question about parts, an agent can readily tap into inventory information to find the answer. Because agents have access to a wealth of information, each agent can perform multiple tasks. They can resolve each issue quickly and accurately with a single call, increasing their potential for up-selling or cross-selling.

The functionality needed to succeed in customer support includes call-center and online support, field-service scheduling and dispatching, and wireless field service. It demands complete views of spare parts availability, logistics, service billing, and customer contract entitlements.

The first step in increasing the size and efficiency of support activities is to make as many of them as possible self-service. Most companies use employee/customer interactions for support activities that could be handled faster and more efficiently with self-service Web sites. Many support calls require customers to navigate maze-like phone trees of ever-increasing complexity and ever-decreasing performance, set up to "better serve the customers." A company may regard the support call as beginning when a support agent picks up the phone; for the customer, however, it begins at the first prompt, and it may end before human contact is made. Have you tried to call a bank lately? Or to get some simple answer from your health care provider? Be forewarned: the menu options have changed. Self-service should be a way of providing service, not of avoiding contact.

The implementation of self-service begins with compiling what a company already knows and getting it online. Give customers the opportunity to solve as many problems as possible on their own. Installation, configuration, troubleshooting, product availability, price—

what information do customers want? Make it available, and keep it current. Remove information that is no longer valid, and make sure that new information is immediately available. Credibility rests on responsiveness. All your processes need to move at Internet speed.

Consider the activities that customers could perform without human assistance—if only companies would enable them to

- Ask questions or search a knowledge base
- Learn from other customers
- Download information
- Apply for credit
- Request service
- Maintain personal data
- Select collateral, information, and/or merchandise to be sent
- Personalize service agreements
- Register for events
- Renew orders (for magazines, for checks, etc.)
- Renew warranties
- Review account statuses or balances
- Review billing information
- Update installed-base information

Self-service provides a tremendous opportunity to collect data on customer activity. The means to do so—and to turn the data into meaningful information—must be integrated with your self-service applications. Never has it been more important for business intelligence applications to be part of core business processes. A prerequisite of rapid response is the ability to receive and act on information in real time.

Globalizing Software

"Globalizing software" can mean any of a number of things. But using globalized software to run a global company means something fairly specific. Recapitulating to some extent, let's pin down that meaning.

The company must have access to the global network that the Internet constitutes. It must maintain a single central database that serves as the foundation for a single global instance of the company's software. The software must automate corporate business processes that span all its lines of business (marketing, sales, service, financials, HR, procurement, etc.) and support all the channels (face-to-face, Web, interaction centers, etc.) through which that business is conducted. The database must maintain a single comprehensive record for every member of the company's trading community: its customers, its employees, its business partners, the members of its supply and demand chains. The software must accommodate business in all major languages and all major currencies, and it must address all contracting needs, all major tax issues, and all internal financial requirements. Let's look at some financial concerns.

Some Financial Issues

Global commerce presents some financial challenges of special merit, things your accountants and lawyers can sink their teeth into.

Taxes

Death and taxes! The problem of taxes grows more complicated with global commerce (while death remains as simple as ever). Though tax laws must be adhered to, they are often open to interpretation. If you ask two accountants to interpret a given rule, you can expect at least two answers. For global expansion, it is critical to find local people in every region in which you do business who can be trusted to help you sort fact from fiction. Moreover, every multinational needs to use software that codifies the tax considerations that are relevant in each location where it does business.

Charts of Accounts

Charts of accounts (COAs) present the challenge of consolidating results. The varieties of COAs and of accounting rules, together with the multiplicity of currencies, make it hard for accountants to arrive at the point where they can compare apples with apples. As an example, Oracle reconciles the differences with some difficulty, emerging with what it terms *constant dollars*.

Payments

In the United States, almost all dollar transfers are handled by moving paper (e.g., by sending checks). Though this can be done efficiently, it usually is not. In Europe, electronic funds transfer (EFT) is used widely; however, there are more than 150 EFT formats, with more being developed. Every major bank has its own format; even some bank branches do. The communications technology that is used to send EFT files is archaic, amounting to little more than a secured modem connection.

The Close Process

All CEOs and CFOs want daily close numbers. They don't care about the logistics of the process; they just want the numbers. "How are we doing this quarter, with 10 days remaining, as compared to last year, last quarter?" The general ledger tends to be regarded as the source of truth; the problem is that the general ledger is the last station on a lengthy journey—from campaign to lead, from lead to opportunity, from opportunity to quote, from quote to order, then to accounting, finally to the general ledger. Most companies don't even post daily close numbers; without an integrated solution, they can't. If you do business globally, the consolidation problems make the close problem even more complex. If you aren't running integrated software from a single instance, daily close numbers based on daily information will never even be a gleam in your accountant's eye.

Corporate Structure and Tax Liability

The legal structure a company establishes determines how it can move profits among countries or regions to gain tax advantages—the idea being to create the most profit in locations where taxes are low. For example, a company could manufacture something in one subsidiary, sell it to another at a small profit, sell it to a third subsidiary in a region with favorable taxes at a large profit, and finally sell it to a customer at a small profit. However, to make this work, the systems that perform internal bookkeeping must handle multiple organizations cost-effectively. Sending invoices and receipts slowly back and forth among subsidiaries can easily eat up profits. Handling of transactions between and among organizations is an important issue for business software, one that has only recently been addressed in the application marketplace.

Invoicing

Some customers require consecutive invoice numbers, imposing on their vendors the need to reserve ranges of numbers. Invoices that are consecutive in number may also be required to be consecutive in date and time, and may be subjected to sequencing by region and type as well. Such requirements can be especially strict in relation to service-contract renewals.

Rules for revenue recognition vary from one country to another. Some countries make it legal to invoice prior to the start date of a service; in others it is forbidden to do so. Some customers are exempt from taxes. Some may want to see quotes in U.S. dollars but to be invoiced in the local currency; such arrangements may require that the vendor's system have the ability to lock in the exchange rate that obtains at the time of quoting.

Contracts

We have seen (in the section "Obligations" in Chap. 3) that contracts come in an assortment of flavors. The global enterprise confronts the need to take contracts global to the extent allowed by circumstances— but that extent is hard to identify. Is there such a thing as a global contract?

Existing software automates service renewals, warranties, sales orders, and purchase agreements within distinct countries. But this limitation can be a serious inconvenience to the relationship between any two far-flung multinationals. Is it possible for a single contract to govern any major area of the dealings between two such companies in a way that is valid for all the countries in which they do business? Possibly so; but such a contract would presumably have to incorporate

- Price lists that might vary from one country or group of countries to another
- Tax stipulations that would so vary
- Legal obligations that might need to be sensitive to discrepancies in national laws
- Other terms and conditions that might vary from country to country
- Currency and conversion provisions for multiple currencies

- Sales credit obligations, rights, royalties, and other matters that might vary across borders

The range of complexities is such that "the global contract," still hypothetical, may remain so forever.

Summary

The requirements of successful participation in global markets are also those of a rapid-response enterprise. Companies must have the goal of running their applications from a single global instance, embodying an infrastructure of business practices that support global operations. IT must be more powerful and yet smaller, operating largely in the "human-free" zone. True e-business processes must be more integrated with each other, cover more situations, and result in more information for decision making. These business processes must be automated, and the outward-facing processes (selling, buying, customer service) must be automated first, with thought given to the business identity being presented. Global business processes must be implemented with globalized business software that can handle multiple languages, currencies, file formats, laws, and other cultural and regional differences.

Mission-critical activities must be available around the clock and around the globe. Operating 24 × 7 means that the IT maintenance window is small; adjustments such as software upgrades and procedural changes need to happen quickly, with minimal impact on staff and none on customers.

A global e-business needs to be faster—and to meet higher expectations. It needs to respond quickly to changes in the market by responding quickly to decisions from its C-level executives. The key to meeting these needs is to eliminate complexity wherever possible; where this is *not* possible, the impact of complexity on the business must be buffered by deploying automation to address and constrain it. Simplicity and responsiveness = survival and success.

5
Management by Fact

Dead . . . wrong! That's what the executive was . . . [1]

How much time have *you* spent in high-level corporate meetings debating whether "the numbers" are right? Megawatts of corporate effort have been spent on "analysis" of corporate numbers that is really nothing more than glorified summarization for executives on the next-higher rung of the corporate ladder; and if those executives don't like the summaries presented, they often spend much of *their* time persuading themselves that the numbers must be mistaken.

The brightest, most thoughtful, most industrious, and most credible of senior executives can make terrible decisions, sometimes cataclysmic ones, because the information they have is wrong. Others, probably not the most credible, can distort information for personal gain. Such things can happen when the facts are in doubt, or when they are overridden by personality. Moving toward rapid response means managing by facts—facts provided by corporate computer systems.

A major purpose of any respectable suite of business software must be to expose the facts. To do so, the suite must

- Be comprehensive, enabling all relevant business areas
- Be global in scope
- Be founded on a single base of reconciled and well-organized data
- Provide statistical analysis and knowledge management that can convert data into business intelligence

[1]A tip of the hat here to James Thurber

■ Grant executives self-service access to that business intelligence

Some will say that if all the data are in one place, it is a trivial matter to get information out. I agree, but saying this begs the important question. In the first place, getting all the *needed* data in is a major challenge; it's also a perpetual challenge, because business intelligence will continually raise questions whose answers require data not yet collected. Often, needed attributes of certain data, or crucial relationships among them, have not been recorded. Moreover, the ability to work productively with the data collected depends heavily on how those data are organized; much planning is needed to design data structures that both accept data efficiently and yield data gracefully for analysis. So getting reliable information out is nontrivial. Many enterprises migrating from traditional to electronic modes of business will carry with them the contaminated data of the past—incomplete, inconsistent, contradictory, false. Such a business will need industrial-strength mechanisms to scrub and rationalize such data.

Perhaps the most promising method is for the business to enable every other entity in its universe—every employee, business partner, supply-chain member, customer—to maintain its own data. No matter how eager a business may be to keep its data reliable, somebody else is often the source of truth—and usually has a motive to spread that truth. Beyond this, many businesses will begin to employ data librarians whose job will be to keep customer, product, installed-base, and marketing data clean and reliable.

Another crucial hurdle on the path to potent business information is the implementation of business processes that are simple and easy to understand. The more radically an e-business suite is customized to suit the enterprise using it, the more complex and unreliable it will grow. Business information can still be extracted from it, perhaps in a form that the users find more familiar and more congenial; but the substance of that information is likely to be more intricate and more difficult to construe correctly.

Luckily, the use of an e-business suite begins the revolution of a virtuous circle. The more fully the suite is deployed, the more usable information can be extracted. (Product A collects its own data, but the addition of product B means that the system can now generate not only data collected by product B—as well as data collected by product

A—but information also about how the products, and the entities they relate to, interact.) The more the senior executives use the suite's business intelligence (BI) facilities, the easier they will find them—or make them—to use. The simpler the company's processes, the more reliable and understandable the data they generate; and such data will often serve to make the business processes still simpler and more efficient. This cyclical process is the heart of management by fact.

What business view—if any—do your C-level executives use habitually as a home page? In fact, there is a widespread drought of business intelligence at the levels where those executives need it, and the consequence is that many of them don't have home pages or don't care about the home pages they've been offered. But the growing need for rapid response will challenge top executives to begin using e-business suites that feature sophisticated methods for business-data analysis.

A serviceable e-business home page will be configurable to offer the information that the executive viewer considers most important for his work. The user interface can be divided, in effect, into a number of rectangular "bins," each presenting a number of line items detailing (often quantitatively) the status of the company or of a specific line of business; the state of the art enables the viewer to select among a large number of bins and to define the locations in which the bins chosen are to appear on the display. Each line item should constitute a link, so that the viewer can click on it to invoke a display of more—and more detailed—information for the item. The home page is likely to include other more general links, each leading to a high-level screen summarizing an important aspect of operations. This use of links enables executive viewers, through self-service in real time, to drill down into global transaction data to view key performance indicators that reveal the health and operations of the business.

The Five Phases

As I view it, management by fact is enabled by a cycle that has five phases (as shown in Fig. 5-1). Each phase is a process, and the five may all be proceeding simultaneously. To some extent they overlap, but the important point is that the impetus developed by any one phase is passed on to the next, by which—ideally—it will be amplified.

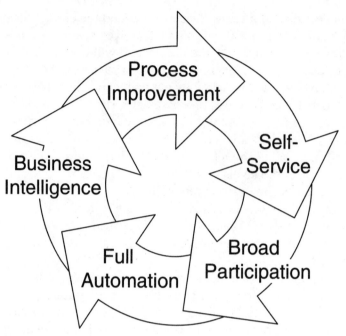

Figure 5-1. Management by Fact: The Virtuous Circle

Once the cycle is well begun, every entry point makes as much sense as every other one. For discussion's sake, however, it makes sense to begin with self-service.

Self-Service

We've touched several times on the advantages of self-service systems, but it won't hurt to review and synopsize them at this point. Such systems enable everyone with access to the Internet to

- Perform the desired function at any time
- Perform it from any place
- Bypass administrative staff, reducing expenses for the site sponsor and saving time on both ends
- Retain responsibility for the user's own data, keeping those data under the control of the person with the greatest relevant concern and understanding
- Avoid communications costs

In doing these things, these systems confer an additional benefit on both the site sponsor and the user: they provide a seductive opportunity for the user to learn more about the sponsor's business.

Broad Participation

Self-service will obviously spread direct participation in virtually every business that implements it, sometimes by several orders of magnitude. The advantages for the business are tremendous: increased customer satisfaction, reduced administrative time and expenses, reduced communications costs, and heightened data accuracy (with a concomitant reduction in miscommunications, misunderstandings, and service errors, meaning reductions in merchandise returns and even in litigation).

Full Automation

Self-service and broader participation in the business both argue in favor of full automation. The magnified flow of data into the system not only increases the rewards to be gained by automating its processing; it also imposes greater penalties on businesses that cannot sustain automated business flows. Sometimes such interruptions take place because business processes still require physical labor; sometimes they happen because the flow of information depends on human involvement, and the job required is done at human speed or—when there's nobody to do it—not at all.

This is not to recommend that every business—or even any business—aim for zero headcount. *Full automation* means automating every function that it is cost-effective to automate. Though the range of such functions is constantly increasing, there will always be some business functions in which human involvement is a strategic necessity.

Business Intelligence

Data flowing into a computer system are essential to any business intelligence that that system can generate. Broad participation in the system, driven by self-service functionality, thus can help to augment and to refine business intelligence, improving its accuracy and reliability at the same time as it lowers its cost. Full automation clearly brings a further contribution, extending the possible sources of relevant data and cutting the time and expense required to subject those data to business analysis.

In this respect, the ideal business runs a fully automated transactional system that is self-service, real-time, and global. Sophisticated BIS software empowered by such a system can generate invaluable insights into business strategy, arming executives to manage by fact and to implement rapid response. Changes in compensation plans, in product prices, in marketing budget allocations, in siting plans, in benefit offerings—indeed, in almost any major business concern—can be the logical outcome of the numbers that a business intelligence system can generate.

Process Improvement

Process improvement is the goal of such changes—and usually the result. Process improvement does not just mean changes of course; overwhelmingly, it means simplification, which should lead in general to faster and more reliable executive decisions.

Room for improvement is the biggest room in the world, and it's certainly big enough in systems for business automation. These began with some 25 years of mainframe computing, characterized by arcane proprietary programs, by exclusion of users from the process, by unforgiving user interfaces (UIs), and by spotty automation—the Stone Age of computers. Then followed the Iron Age: 10 years of client/server systems, local and distributed, with data and processes still fragmented, on a variety of platforms; computer initiates were still the only ones with meaningful access to the systems. The legacy of those 35 years is a Tower of Babel: layer upon layer of platforms, databases, systems interfaces, and UIs, with data and computer-science skills fragmented and ill coordinated. This legacy has been bequeathed from CIO to CIO as if it were a palace of wisdom, designed by an organizational genius and constructed by legendary engineers. It is a kludge.

Or it was. The Internet, and the changes it has brought, has equipped us to throw out that legacy and replace it with something that seems, by comparison, like Bach contrasted with Meat Loaf.

(Some will consider my view of the current state of things too harsh. I invite them to meditate on the system of one Oracle customer, a leading provider of computer components—illustrated in Fig. 5-2—and to bear in mind that the diagram [already!] reflects the

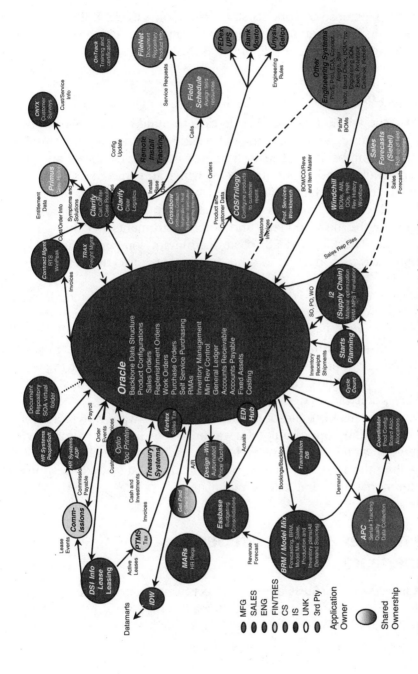

Figure 5-2. One Oracle Customer's Software System—after Substantial Rationalization

105

results of extensive work to standardize on Oracle ERP products. Figure 5-3, representing an anticipated future configuration, reflects a standardization on the full Oracle E-Business Suite.)

And in Conclusion

In fact, the whole five-phase cycle calls to mind the development of classical music, which began with crude instruments and simple-minded compositions. The instruments made ugly noises and got tuned. They found wider audiences, which in some cases (e.g., the shawm, the glass harmonica) voted with their feet; in other cases (e.g., the clavier/piano) inventors made improvements, composers wrote for the new models, and some instruments became global standards. The life or death of an instrument sometimes turned on whether it was congenial to other instruments or to the orchestra as a whole.

Meanwhile the art of composition was developing too. It was moving toward greater complexity, to be sure, but ideally toward complexity that was well organized, widely resourceful, and—most important—subordinated to the effect the music was designed to have on its "users," the audience. Many would argue that the 20th century saw classical composition pass way beyond that ideal, just as business software systems did.

Whatever may be said of music, business software now confronts an outstanding opportunity for rational reform. That reform will emerge from the five-phase cycle, with each phase leading into and impelling the next, and the whole evolving organically in response to the momentum gradually accumulated.

Companies and the Self-Service Experience

Virtually every business needs to direct its attention to the members of four categories: its business partners, its employees, its customers, and its suppliers. Together, these make up the business's trading community. For each of these categories in turn, this section considers what the ideal self-service experience would be.

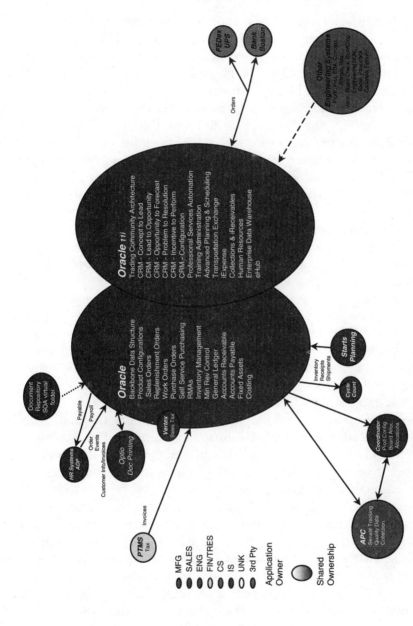

Figure 5-3. The Same System after Projected Standardization on the Oracle E-Business Suite

107

Ideal Self-Service: Business Partners

Business partners include value-added resellers (VARs), value-added distributors (VADs), and channel partners of various kinds. They may also include co-developers of technology or other products. A very basic business-partner flow is illustrated in Fig. 5-4; most site sponsors will provide far more functionality than is shown here.

For business partners, the first logical step toward doing electronic business with a site sponsor is to pass through a self-service registration process that calls for all basic information that the sponsor needs in order to conduct such business. For every business partner, a single ID and password may be initialized; multiple sets will be allowed when the sponsor needs to distinguish among departments or specific employees of the partner company. Telephone numbers, e-addresses, and shipping addresses will be entered in most cases; areas of interest may be solicited. Recognized site users will be empowered to maintain their own data, adding simplicity and accuracy to the update process.

Once registered, a user will be granted access to the site's knowledge-management features. The site may actively push promotional information to users; in any case, most business sites will provide search facilities by which users can locate products or services of interest and information relating to them. Intranet search engines will promote call avoidance for the site sponsor, reducing business expenses while increasing user satisfaction.

User privileges will include direct access to lists or catalogs of products and services offered. Information gathered by this means will enable them to make selections; they can then proceed to the sponsor's Internet store in order to price and purchase the offerings selected. Once an order is entered, the user responsible will be able to inquire as to its status. The site will include a payment mechanism supporting payments by electronic data interchange (EDI), electronic funds transfer (EFT), and credit cards, as well as payments related to outstanding purchase orders. It will provide directions for paying by cash or check.

Sites will provide postsale support by enabling users to enter requests for technical assistance; a statusing feature will again be supplied, allowing the user to track the sponsor's reaction to such requests. Many sites, particularly those of large high-tech companies, will conduct ongoing forums and threaded discussions through

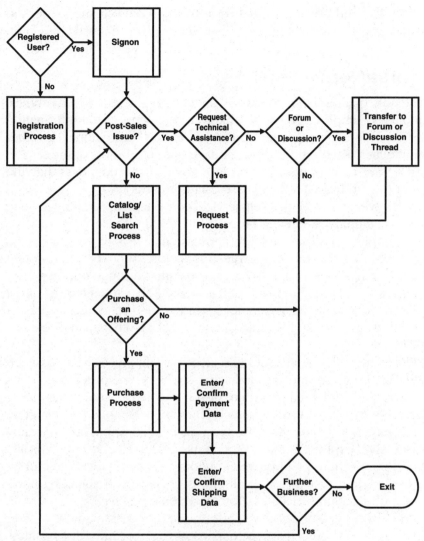

Figure 5-4. A Web-Site Business Flow for Business Partners

which users can exchange tips and can pose and/or answer technical questions.

The ideal site will also provide a renewal feature for ongoing services, including warranties, subscriptions, and contracts. More sophisticated versions of the renewal mechanism may include the ability to send advance notice of a renewal date to the associated e-address or to allow the subscriber to authorize renewal by default.

Ideal Self-Service: Employees

The fully qualified e-business will maintain online employee profiles, and every employee must be able to access most of the information in his or her own profile and much of the information for other employees. Each employee must have control of most of the data in his or her own profile, on the grounds that the employee has the most to gain from keeping those data accurate.

However, most of the self-service performed by employees will involve employee benefit programs. Typically these programs are fully public, so all information about them needs to be online and accessible to the full employee population. Such programs often include employee stock purchases, sometimes through option grants; in such cases an employee self-service Web site needs to show information on shares accumulated and vesting schedules, or needs to link to the site of a business partner that administers the relevant programs.

Other money-related issues of concern to employees include direct-deposit programs and tax deductions, which employees should be empowered to configure within legal limits. Because they also incur business expenses, employees need a simple method for reporting such expenses online and for securing needed approvals. In many cases, such expenses are for procurement; e-companies will typically have one or more preapproved vendors for every type of item to be procured, and they will typically have preapproved spending limits and authorization procedures for exceptional purchases.

Employees must be able to perform such processes quickly and to get reimbursed quickly. Some expenses—notably those for business travel—are important enough to justify online definition and automated enforcement of spending policies. At Oracle, for instance, employees use etravel.com to make plane, hotel, and car reservations; by defining and enforcing rules and policies governing such reservations, the company has saved 18 percent of all travel-related expenses, amounting to $14 million per year.

Needless to add, business expenses lead sometimes to disputes, for which every company needs a rapid and just dispute-resolution process. Such processes also can be advanced to some extent by the use of software.

Another area suited to employee self-service is time management, which may or may not be money-related. Some or all employees may be required to record time worked for payroll purposes, for more general accounting purposes, or for project management purposes. At a minimum, employees are normally expected to record exceptions—sick days, holidays, and the like—to a default work schedule. Every e-business uses software to support employee entry of time records; the software will check the data entered for plausibility, but the employee is generally treated as the ranking authority on how his or her work time has been spent.

More broadly construed, time management includes scheduling. Employees need automated support for maintaining personal work calendars, and they can work more effectively if they are provided with programs that support group and project scheduling, not to mention the scheduling of conference calls, meeting rooms, and so on.

Employee self-service needs to approach the ideal suggested here if the employing company is to operate at reasonable efficiency. But even the smallest step toward automating employee self-service can be an enormous gain for both the employee, who will feel (and be) empowered, and the employer, which will typically be able to displace tedious clerical paperwork, often on a grand scale, and at the same time slash data-entry and data-reproduction errors to the bone.

Ideal Self-Service: Customers

For any company in the *Fortune* 500, its principal Web site must be intuitive, compelling, and complete. Here *intuitive* means easy to use: there is no training manual for amazon.com or yahoo.com. Moreover, the principal Web site must exploit the company's brand identity, not confuse or dilute it. That's why Cisco offers cisco.com, Microsoft offers microsoft.net, Oracle offers oracle.com, SAP offers MySAP.com, and Siebel offers siebel.com.

The Marketing and Sales Phases
Commercial traffic in general can be generated by ads in various media: TV, radio, Web sites, and others. Electronic traffic in particular can be generated by campaigns, promotions, prompts for service or

warranty renewals, and outbound e-mail broadsides for new products, features, and services. Press releases can point readers to a URL that serves as a "landing pad"; viewers accessing the URL can then register, as appropriate, and move on to a customer information portal.

The principal Web site should make available all company-standard products, services, prices, and configurations. It needs to be coordinated with the company's catalog, with its interaction center(s), and with its retail channel in order to ensure that the customer's experience with the company is consistent and reliable. Business strategy may justify *some* exceptions, however; for instance, the company may offer some of its products only through its Web store.

Customers should find that, once they have identified the products they want, they can order all of those products and they can review the status of any outstanding order. Under some circumstances, specific and dedicated price lists must be visible, and their provisions must be applied reliably; otherwise the site must apply standard pricing. In either case it must calculate and impose appropriate charges for taxes and shipping. The site must accept, but not require, online payment by credit card, purchase order, or line of credit. Physical shipping must follow, usually offline, accompanied by invoicing and cash receipt from customers that have not paid online.

The Service Phase

At this point the marketing and sales cycles are complete. Setting aside further such cycles, what follows now is service and customer care. This phase logically begins with the enablement of returns, for which the ideal Web site also will provide comprehensive support. It may allow customers to print bar codes and/or shipping labels to be used with return merchandise, and it should supply a call-center number or direct customers through a Web procedure to contact an interaction center.

The customer-support phase can be extensive and complex, befitting the fact that it may last as long as the most dependable company product—or longer. From the outset, the customer may have questions about product configurations and compatibilities, although the ideal site will try to preempt as many of these as possible through the provision of frequently asked questions (FAQs) and, where appropriate, of one or more configuration applications. Many products will engender setup questions, which may also be addressed through FAQs. Customers with questions that don't qualify as "frequent" may want to search a knowledge base or join a forum or threaded discussion. Though they may be helped by ad hoc online learning, some will probably take an interest in whatever formal training the company provides and will want to be able to consult an online calendar of marketing events, courses, and seminars.

Despite all such support, some customers will still need to log problem tickets. The first agent a customer speaks to may not be able to solve the problem in question, and the agent may arrange a Web-based collaboration session to clarify further the problem or its resolution. Such a session, if conducted, may still fail to solve the problem; if so, an engineer may be assigned and/or a field sales representative (FSR) dispatched. In either case—if the experience is ideal—the problem will at last be resolved and the trouble ticket closed.

No customer wants to encounter problems in setting up or using a company's products. Ideally, the products will be flawless in every respect, but bringing products to that exalted level is the concern of manufacturing and the software that supports it. The business of CRM software is to ensure that any problems generated by imperfect products cause as little annoyance as possible to users of those products. This means that such software must enable a support process that is broad, deep, and flexible—a process that allows the customer as many avenues of recourse as it can, within reason, and that not only helps the customer to pursue those avenues but guides that pursuit, as appropriate, starting with resources that are less costly to the company and moving when necessary to those that are more costly, always with provision for rapid sharp escalations depending on the importance of the problem and/or the customer.

Ideal Self-Service: Suppliers

With respect to self-service, suppliers make up the odd category within the trading community. Here the ideal self-service is offered not *to* them but *by* them.

Instead of registering with the companies they supply, suppliers of business equipment and services will generally maintain product catalogs on their own sites, which may be restricted to certified buyers or may be open to all viewers who are willing to register. An alternative is presented by some third-party sites that serve as catalog aggregators, allowing businesses that are looking for supplies to search multiple catalogs simultaneously and to compare prices.

Major consumers of business supplies will generally maintain internal lists of authorized suppliers. An employee who has identified a supply need, or who is working with a compiled list of needed items, will initiate the procurement cycle by logging on to the site of a supplier or of a catalog aggregator. Prospective purchases in major volumes or of expensive goods will typically trigger one or more negotiation sessions, for which the parties involved need systems providing fully enabled Internet support—in many cases employing voice over Internet Protocol (VoIP) technology.

Once both parties have agreed on terms, the purchasing process will generally follow a simple and familiar flow, including shipping, invoicing, and collection by the supplier and payment and receipt of goods by the company supplied. The entire process, except for physical delivery of the goods, will almost always be automated, using options for shipment and payment that have been selected in advance by the purchasing company. The basic flow is shown in Fig. 5-5.

The Revenue Portal: Self-Service for Executives

Top-level executives need—and want—to be self-sufficient. The Internet caters to this concern—one of the many reasons that make Internet applications compelling. Given a crack at Yahoo! or myCFO.com or economist.com, execs do not look around for a training manual; they simply use the site. If and when the site ceases to be useful for them, they can find others.

Almost all top business executives focus on the sales life cycle, which is traditionally shown as a funnel (Fig. 5-6). In fact, the general popularity of this view of a company's business will lead quickly to fairly standardized Web portals for C-level executives. Through such revenue portals they will be able to examine each of the six major stages of the cycle.

Responses. The executive wants to know:

- How many responses are being generated by the company's marketing initiatives

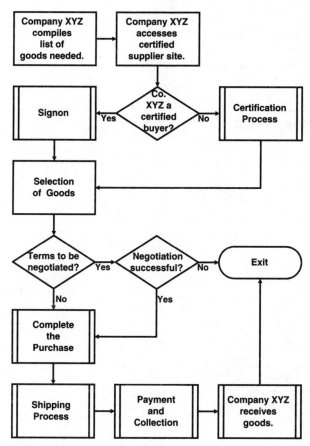

Figure 5-5. Self-Service Flow on Supplier Site

- The profiles or characteristics of the businesses or consumers that are responding
- What specific collateral, ads, or demos are eliciting responses
- What products and/or services the responses are targeting
- And so on

Leads. These are an early—and in some ways the most important—indicator of a company's health. Using a respectable e-business suite, the executive can now see what proportion of responses turn into leads, which segments of respondents are generating leads at higher rates, how well company staff are qualifying the leads generated, to which country organizations or branches the leads are being assigned, etc.

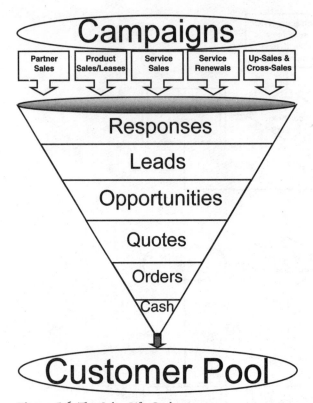

Figure 5-6. The Sales Life Cycle

Opportunities. Crucial, again, is the proportion of leads that become opportunities. Moreover, opportunities are the basis for sales forecasts, so not only their dollar volume but their quality is vitally important. On a more detailed level, the executive needs to know what business is closing today, whether it was won or lost, and what the hot possibilities are for the fortnight to come. Do sales reps' opportunity figures jibe with those of the management team?

Quotes. Once more: how do quote dollar totals compare to opportunity dollar totals? Quoting is moving rapidly into the new world of self-service. Sales reps may turn opportunity data into quotes; quotes may be automatically generated from corporate master contracts; discounts are applied as appropriate. Or quotes may be issued to customers through a Web store; the customers then review and approve the quotes, the approved quotes pass as necessary through internal review processes, and sales credits are automatically assigned. Quote totals feed back into the cycle to help refine sales forecasts.

Orders. Orders can be enormously complex, and there are limits to what can helpfully be said about them outside the context of a specific industry. But characteristics that are important almost universally include these:

- How many lines does the average order contain, and what is the range?
- How are ordered products configured?
- How are they to be shipped and paid for?
- What proportion of the order's total is earned and what proportion is unearned revenue?
- What proportion of earned revenue is recognizable?

The executive can obtain all such information, and far more, using a reasonably competent e-business suite.

Cash. How much cash has come in? Are payments being made by check, by credit card, by EFT, or even in greenbacks? (In any case, the process needs to be integrated with your Web site for cases where that is used and, more generally, with your e-business suite.) Are some payments being deferred until additional products are shipped or services rendered? What amounts are in dispute? (Collection processes generally center on disputed invoice line items, not on the purchaser's financial health or general willingness to pay.)

That is the revenue portal. It enables full self-service by top executives, who can use it to run their companies the way a pilot flies a plane. The instruments support and encourage sensible decisions, taken with confidence and implemented rapidly. The effects of changes will become visible in short order, enabling those changes to be evaluated and providing factual evidence—on which further decisions can be based.

6

Company-to-Company Networking

In Zeno's paradox of Achilles and the tortoise, Achilles can never catch the tortoise—or so it appears—because he must first cover half of the distance of the tortoise's head start, but meanwhile the tortoise is moving ahead. Achilles must then cover half the distance to the tortoise, but meanwhile the tortoise is moving ahead. And so on, *in perpetuum*.

Luckily for software vendors, the situation for business software looks much the same. Perhaps only a finite amount of software is truly "needed," but who can really say? Once the need for ERP applications was met, ERP looked like only half the problem. Now that CRM software is coming to market, the self-dependent enterprise looks like only half the problem. It seems as if there's always another half to be addressed, and the half outstanding at this time is the extraprise: the challenge of helping businesses to be interdependent, to coordinate the work of business B with every other business in B's supply chain—*and* in its demand chain, *and* in its constellation of business partners. Every major business has always necessarily dealt with many others, and it's intuitively clear that making interbusiness dealings efficient poses in some respects a much greater challenge than that of making any business internally efficient.[1]

Once again, the Internet provides the foundation that will enable software companies to meet this challenge. E-business suites built on

---

[1]Still another major challenge for business software—maybe the next half-of-a-half—emerges from the fact that the focus thus far for both ERP and CRM has been on the automation of transactions. The necessary complement is automation of analytics, meaning the development—and pervasive integration with transactional systems—of business intelligence applications.

that foundation are now emerging; they will provide the springboard for rapid response by which companies can interrelate fruitfully to solve the major business problems of the 21st century.[2] Intercompany networking has three major aspects: distance learning, data sharing, and transaction-closure issues. I'll deal with them one by one.

Distance Learning

Distance learning includes communications that are one-to-one, one-to-many, and many-to-many. Telephone conversations have been with us for more than a century, but these have been augmented recently by several technologies mediated by the Internet. These include telephony itself, which voice over Internet Protocol (VoIP) technology has freed from the telephone networks; they also include the provision of Web-site material, which may be fully public or accessible only by authorized viewers. The information itself can be broadcast, or accessed ad hoc, on demand, or in a classroom-like setting. Other techniques supporting distance learning include Internet chat and the use of surveys; they extend further still, to URL sharing and whiteboarding.

(URL sharing is a technique, using Java applets, by which a service rep can direct a caller's browser to an Internet page that appears simultaneously on the agent's screen; a more sophisticated level of URL sharing enables the agent to fill in data on one screen and have the data appear simultaneously on both screens. Whiteboarding enables the agent to paint or draw on both screens simultaneously, as if doing a demo using flip charts. Each technique allows control to be shared, or simply ceded to the caller.)

Whatever the technology and circumstances, the point of distance learning is not to eliminate face-to-face interaction, which indeed is now an option for Internet telephony. It is to eliminate the requirement that the person(s) providing the information share a physical location with the person(s) receiving it, and thus to eliminate travel expenses—for airfare, car rentals, lodging, meals—that in the

[2]The process will be hastened by the work of the Open Applications Group (OAG, at www.openapplications.org). The OAG states its mission as follows: "To define and encourage the adoption of a unifying standard for eBusiness and Application Software interoperability that reduces customer cost and time to deploy solutions."

past have often been unavoidable and cumulatively tremendous. Distance learning can often be accomplished for less than 1 percent of the cost that would once have been required. Its advantages include complete flexibility of time and place: sessions can be recorded and played back as desired, and the most qualified training talent can be exploited without anybody being required to travel.

Consulting

No longer need a company fly a team of consultants from San Francisco to New York City for a one-day seminar on business process reengineering; the same objective can now be accomplished over the Internet. Not only does this save money, but it often means that scheduling flexibility is greatly increased, which makes it easier to assign the most effective consultants to the task and to enroll in the audience the largest number of people who can profit by "attending." Moreover, sessions of this kind can typically be recorded and played back on demand, also over the Internet.

Training

Companies with large sales forces traditionally have held kickoff meetings once a quarter or twice a year that all sales reps are expected to attend. Such meetings were once necessary in order to communicate information, direction, and inspiration to the entire sales force, but bringing the sales reps together from all across the country, or the continent, or beyond, typically represented a major corporate expense.

Distance learning, using the technologies described previously, makes such conventions unnecessary. No longer need a company fly its sales teams from New York City, Chicago, Atlanta, Montreal, and other big cities to Las Vegas so that they can assemble in one huge room to watch motivational movies and listen to speakers. Very similar goals can be achieved without requiring anybody to travel.

These benefits are not confined to mass meetings. Sales professionals who used to spend most of their time on the road can now discharge many of their responsibilities, including checking in with corporate headquarters, without ever boarding a plane. As a result, they can manage their time more effectively; they can arrange for additional product training to fill in gaps in their schedules, and they can absorb direction and product information exactly when it is most needed—when they are first hired or when their assignments are changed.

Teaching

Readers can infer from the previous sections how the Internet can be used to obviate travel for corporate courses. In an earlier generation, computer-based "self study" courses made it possible for employees to absorb some of their training as their other responsibilities allowed, without the direct involvement of a teacher; but students were very much on their own when they had questions about the material or encountered technical or logical difficulties. Internet conferencing techniques mean that study can now take place in a setting that is logically equivalent to a classroom, with the students being able to interact with one another directly, and with or without a teacher's involvement as the sponsoring organization judges desirable.

Perhaps the only serious drawback to such courses arises when a teacher is clearly needed and is not available. However, companies can avoid this situation by giving the students a phone number at which a teacher or adviser can reliably be reached; such an arrangement would relieve the contact person of any need to take direct part in the online activities. On the other hand, use of the Internet means that it is easier to schedule the availability, as teachers or advisers, of the most competent subject-matter experts. The potential quality of the courses rises even as the associated expenses decline.

Product Design

Over the last 30 years, CAD/CAM technology has revolutionized product design across a wide range of industries. But the use of PCs and computer workstations for product design lends itself without difficulty to Internet implementation, which in turn enables collaborative design efforts across arbitrary geographical distances. And, of course, such collaboration is not limited to computer-aided design;

simple pencil drawings can now be transmitted and shared in real time by virtue of URL sharing and whiteboarding technology. So can product plans, engineering documents, and schematics. The subjects of such exchanges can be computer software, aircraft engines, medical equipment, plant maintenance procedures, beer-brewing process models, brand promotions, marketing lists, corn flakes. The possibilities are without limit.

Product Demos

In a number of industries, there may still be a need to conduct many product demos in the physical presence of the audience. But this is clearly no longer true for computer software. The traditional model for software demos is faulty in three major respects:

1. Demos have traditionally been conducted by salespeople without the involvement of the product experts—that is, the programmers.
2. Demos have traditionally been scheduled on demand, with the effect being a tendency for every demo to be unique.
3. By the same token, and because demos may be given at prospects' locations, each demo tends to take place within a novel technical environment.

Each of these factors works against the reliability and the effectiveness of the demo.

Collaborative distance learning techniques make it easier for the software experts to conduct their own demos, according to predetermined schedules. Demos can much more easily be standardized, meaning that their costs can be driven down while both their reliability and their effectiveness are enhanced.

Data Sharing
EDI

For practical purposes, data sharing began in the 1960s, and thus predates the earliest exchanges on the Internet. Early electronic exchanges of data were motivated by the perception that time, effort, and paper could be saved, and mistakes avoided, by finding a way for computers at two or more companies to speak to each other. But the earliest formats for data exchange, emerging as they did from agreements between two business partners, remained local and proprietary. Among the first electronic documents were bills of lading, invoices, and purchase orders.

Data sharing along these lines took on the name *electronic data interchange* (EDI). As time passed, broader standards began to develop within certain industries, including transportation and financial services. However, exchanges between a company in one industry and a company in another industry were generally impossible because of conflicts among industry standards. This problem led to the formation, in 1979, of the ANSI Accredited Standards Committee X12, which was charged with developing a generic standard for EDI.

The result, which reflected the committee's just concern with reliability and security, was solid and effective; it was also very expensive and inflexible. Companies still could not communicate data to each other unless they either were directly linked by leased or dedicated phone lines or belonged to a value-added network (VAN); VANs were proprietary and were sponsored by big companies, including AT&T and IBM. Implementation of EDI at Company XYZ did *not* enable it to communicate with Company ABC unless Company ABC not only was using EDI but could link to Company XYZ; because smaller companies generally could not justify the costs of EDI, it was used almost exclusively for data communications between large companies. Some of these companies (Kmart and Wal-Mart are examples) will not do business with companies that do not use EDI; such policies lock the latter out of business opportunities.

In addition to these drawbacks, the X12 standard, which has been dominant in the United States for decades, has been challenged by UN/EDIFACT (United Nations Electronic Data Interchange for Administration, Commerce, and Trade). Though the two standards are coexisting for the moment, the international one is expected to prevail in the long run. In total, some 100,000 U.S. companies use one or both EDI protocols. While this figure sounds like a lot, it should be compared to a rough total (projected from federal data) of 26 million U.S. companies.

ERP II

The simplest intercompany interactions are "mere" exchanges of information. The principal purpose of enterprise resource planning, as its name makes clear, is to plan the resources of an enterprise. It has begun to evolve into *ERP II*, so dubbed by the Gartner Group, which extends the corporate vision up and down the supply chain by enabling companies to share each other's information—e.g., production schedules and inventories. This makes it possible for companies to reduce their inventory levels, and the associated carrying costs, while at the same time avoiding running out of products that may be needed urgently by their customers.

Clearly, this broadening of ERP beyond the company firewall is often essential to achieving high levels of customer service. In this respect it reemphasizes how important it is for Company XYZ to integrate its ERP and CRM systems internally; on the other hand, the broadening itself is impossible without data-representation conventions that extend *beyond* those internal systems to connect with those of the companies with which XYZ's business interweaves. As XYZ moves to exploit the Internet, it is confronted with—and must respond to—ever-increasing pressure for uniform business conventions.

XML on the Net

The title for this section reflects the fact that the burdens imposed by EDI are twofold and call for a twofold solution. The more important part of this solution is the Internet, which very greatly reduces the costs of data exchange. The mere existence of the Internet, however, does not guarantee a standard protocol for such exchange. EDI is being adapted for Internet-based use, but a more comprehensive solution is needed, and Extensible Markup Language (XML) addresses this need. XML supersedes Hypertext Markup Language (HTML), as well as EDI, by enabling far more detailed and discriminating labeling of the data contents of messages; by doing so, it promises to serve as the basis for exchanges that can be understood, in theory, by every business computer linked to the Internet.

I expect that the dominant model for data exchange in the near future will be guaranteed delivery of XML via what we might call

"HASP," a hub-and-spoke pattern on the Internet. The hubs, in this model, will be Internet exchanges, some of them independent enterprises, others sponsored by traditional brick-and-mortar companies; the spokes will be company-specific connections to such exchanges and links *between* exchanges (Fig. 6-1).

How would this model function, once perfected? Simple communications of information would continue to take place over the Internet as they do today; but the cost-effectiveness of e-commerce would be much enhanced as companies found the logical breadth of their business universe exploding. XML would serve to define standard transaction types consisting of standard elements, and its flexibility would enable transactions to be defined with much greater sensitivity.

Suppose Company C wants to place an order. Thanks to XML, the order can now go beyond specifying such things as the color, size, and quantity of the item to be purchased: it can incorporate specifications as to quality levels, or it can stipulate a maximum price to be paid. Company C launches the order on the Internet by dispatching it to Exchange E, of which it is a member (or perhaps the sponsor).

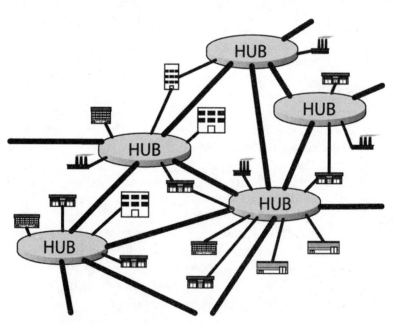

Figure 6-1. The Hub-and-Spoke Pattern for E-Business

Some other member of Exchange E—say Company D—may want to accept the order; but it may have to compete with other companies that are not members of Exchange E, but belong instead to an interacting exchange. Exchange E may accord its own members preferential treatment, but not to the exclusion of the rest of the business universe. Moreover, it may be that *no* member of Exchange E will accept the order as registered. What happens in that case is that XML-sensitive software sponsored by the exchange swings into action, subject to security-related constraints pre-agreed between the exchange and Company C. The software assesses the specifications of the order and decides, again as security concerns allow, to forward it to one or more additional exchanges through which it may plausibly be filled. Eventually Company C's order will arrive at a company, somewhere in the world, that is willing to fill it on the terms that Company C has specified—or, in the worst case, the order will eventually expire, and its failure to find a taker will be reported by Exchange E to the originator.

The difference between the HASP model and EDI is dramatic. Using EDI, a company can send an order to only one other company at a time. In the world of HASP, it expends the same effort to convey the order to the attention, potentially, of every company in the world that may be qualified to fill it. EDI requires direct communication from the first company to the second; HASP takes advantage of zero to many redirections to probe the full scope of the Internet for a favorable response.

Transaction Closure

The ideal for Web-based interactions is that no training manual, and indeed no training, should be necessary. What we have in fact is millions of Web sites that approach this ideal in various degrees; it's intuitively likely that proximity to the ideal generally declines as the functionality of a site increases. In any case, viewers that are new to a site—or even to the Internet—are likely to have more trouble than those who are more experienced.

The upshot is that billions of dollars' worth of business that is begun on the Web, annually, is not completed on the Web—and often is not completed at all. But this is only the beginning of the problem, because many other transactions that might constructively be handled over the Web are subject to the same problems that can derail potential purchases. These include self-service customer care, Web-based education, collaborative product development, and many others.

(I've spent more than an hour on the Web in the last few days trying to find out, using the IRS site, what happened to my 2000 tax refund; toward the end of that time, much of my effort was just a desperate attempt to find out how to speak with a human being. How's that for irony? The Web site finally enables me to buck it off my back and de-automate!)

Our public servants will always be in a class by themselves. But companies that compete in the real world have an acute need to solve such problems before they lose all their customers, and the most reliable solution is to enable the viewer to contact human support. Instead of throwing up their hands and accepting this extremity as a defeat for automation, companies need to simplify and to automate even this process to the extent possible.

This means, above all, giving the viewer an easy way—a *Help* button, for instance—of initiating communication over the Web with a support rep who is qualified to solve all the most common problems. Bypassing complex telephone selection trees, administrative intervention, and support escalations and redirections, direct contact between the person with the problem and the person with the solution is the key to superior customer support over the Internet. Ideally, it will be augmented by capturing as much as possible of the context in which the viewer is operating and conveying the captured information to the support rep.

Once Web-based contact has been established, recently developed collaborative technologies make it easy for support staff to extend effective help to viewers. These technologies include *URL sharing* and *whiteboarding*, both described earlier in this chapter under "Distance Learning." Some of the products that support these techniques allow simultaneous display and update of the screens of typical desktop products, including spreadsheets, word processors, and presentation tools.

Tools like these can be lifelines in cases where viewers have almost despaired of completing the self-service tasks they set out to accomplish. Shopping carts that are about to be abandoned can be rescued, enhancing revenues for the site sponsor and protecting its relationship with the would-be customer. College students can be helped to complete course registration successfully. Viewers who are trying to solve their own technical problems can be given just the boost they need, helping the site sponsor to avoid the much lengthier and more expensive technical support effort that would result if the viewer had to call a support center and try to describe the difficulty encountered.

Summary

Company-to-company networking—at least on the scale enabled by the Internet—is unprecedented. We have examined several of the major benefits it will confer:

- Companies will enjoy greatly expanded access to the internal data of their business partners, enabling them to forecast more reliably and to enhance the efficiencies of their supply and demand chains.
- The finest business and technical talent will become available on demand, with minimal disruption to the sponsoring company, thus enabling new levels of corporate service.
- Training costs will be reduced dramatically on both sides of the teacher-pupil relationship. Expenditures of time and money for training-related travel will be largely swept away. Providers of expertise will increasingly be able to convert corporate expertise and supporting documentation into revenue-generating assets.
- By means of a process we might call "guided closure," greater proportions of transactions will be closed with greater accuracy.

The first two of these changes will drive corporate business competence and innovation, while the third will more directly drive the economy itself by promoting the ability of vendors to sell their goods and of purchasers to identify and acquire the goods they need.

7

Software by Industry

Some software vendors may design their products from the first for use in a specific industry. This allows them to ignore the complications attendant on variations from one industry to another in terminologies, business practices, and focal concerns, but it does so at the cost of limiting potential sales of such products.

The major vendors of business applications—Oracle, PeopleSoft, SAP, and Siebel—have taken a more ambitious approach, which starts with designing products to provide all basic business functionality. After all, the needs and uses for some traditional back-office applications, including those for human resources and accounting purposes, usually vary only slightly from one industry to another. However, because business software *must* solve industry-specific problems in order to find a market, these companies then develop variants of their basic products, each suited to the needs of a specific industry. The central challenge for each company, while developing such variants, is to stick as close as possible to a single code line; doing so minimizes the costs of maintenance and future development and maximizes the leverage the vendor can gain from spanning multiple industries. That leverage is multiplied in some instances by opportunities and complexities shared by two or more industries.

Thus vendors experience an ongoing conflict between the need to tailor their products to specific industries and the need to control their development and maintenance budgets. From this conflict arise such questions as these: What does manufacturing a corn flake have in common with maintaining an aircraft engine? What does leasing a backhoe have in common with administering an MRI scan? What does selling a book on an Internet site have in common with providing prescription-drug samples to physicians? The answers to such questions figure in the calculations of the major providers of business software, which must constantly trade off R&D dollars between generic functionality and industry-specific capabilities.

This chapter will discuss several industries, addressing their distinguishing characteristics and problems. It is not an exhaustive survey; instead, it concentrates on a few industries whose problems have especially interesting implications for business software. In doing so, it will try to convey a sense of what characteristics the breakfast-cereal industry shares with the aircraft industry, and what beer brewers have in common with bankers.

Aviation, Aerospace, and Defense

The aviation, aerospace, and defense (AA&D) industry comprises huge global systems in which manufacturers and operators must integrate procurement with maintenance to generally stringent requirements. The goals, in order of importance, are high reliability, quick turnaround, and low maintenance costs. Such complex equipment as jet engines and airframes has special needs for maintenance, repair, and overhaul (MRO). Application software must address processes unique to the aftermarket service industry and the challenges inherent in maintaining such equipment. Certain outstanding characteristics span the industry:

- Rigid aircraft maintenance requirements designed to ensure the safest possible operation

- Complex equipment configurations with many dependencies governing the usage of parts and assemblies

- Huge amounts of original equipment manufacturer (OEM) and government information that must be kept current and coordinated— and be complied with—to maximize accuracy and efficiency[1]

---

[1]While these requirements present the biggest challenge in this industry, they are shared to some extent by any industry that involves the operation and maintenance of high-value, long-lived assets, such as ships, submarines, railway stock, construction equipment, trucks, public transit vehicles, pipeline pumping stations, power generation systems, and medical diagnostic equipment.

The aircraft maintenance business is growing. The world's airline fleet is expected to add more than 7,000 aircraft by 2010.[2] Aircraft are remaining in service longer, primarily because of improvements in design quality and maintenance practices. Outsourcing of fleet maintenance has become viable, obviating the construction of expensive maintenance facilities by new airlines and allowing them to offer flights much sooner. All of this represents an increase of millions of hours of maintenance activity, and OEMs and airlines have recognized the associated profit opportunities.

With passengers as concerned about on-time departure as about competitive fares, airlines' maintenance operations now compete with one another to achieve high aircraft dispatch rates. Worldwide, however, maintenance facilities are operating at or near capacity. To improve throughput, efficiency must be increased; to increase profitability, costs must be reduced. Technology can provide solutions, but it must be the right technology.

Maintenance vs. Manufacturing

The MRO industry differs fundamentally from conventional manufacturing, as it contains more unknowns and unique situations. Even though much maintenance activity consists of standard checks, the scope of the work and the parts required are often unknown until a unit has been disassembled and inspected. MRO for AA&D is subject to safety standards that are more stringent than those for other types of equipment. For service companies, events such as airworthiness directives from the FAA can result in unplanned jobs requiring quick turnaround, making scheduling and workflow management more difficult.

In a manufacturing environment, parts come from inventory. In a maintenance environment, a replacement part may come from the inventory of the service provider, a third party, or the customer; or the replacement may be effected by redirecting a part from another service job; and the cost of the part may vary according to its source. Identical parts can have different requirements attached to them, depending on the aircraft configuration, the sales order, the scope of work, and industry regulations. Inventory applications for MRO must

[2]This forecast takes into account the current economic slowdown and the effects of the terrorist attack of September 11, 2001.

be able to record times and cycles (takeoffs and landings) for life-limited and time-tracked parts. Material management includes "picking" rules that specify how parts may be selected from inventory. Picking rules can be determined by the customer, by contract, or by product. The more intelligently and accurately the software applies such rules, the more efficient and profitable the process will be. Another key industry-specific inventory function is the ability to select substitute parts: for a specific part in a specific configuration, what alternatives are valid—and, if one is used, how is the configuration affected?

Aircraft parts are expensive, and the importance of keeping planes in the air means that billions of dollars are spent on spare parts inventory. Canceling a single transatlantic flight because of an airworthiness defect can cost an airline as much as $200,000. Airlines alone carry nearly $35 billion in hardware and spare-parts inventory and spend about $10 billion on replenishment purchases annually; military spending may be double or even triple this amount. Whereas the goal in manufacturing is zero inventory, the goal in maintenance is having the right part in the right place at the right time, which has meant carrying large inventories that include very expensive parts. Having access to information about the status of every part, whether flying or on the ground, will open the hangar doors to more efficient short-flow work planning and material management.

Service and service parts are profit makers for companies in AA&D. A large part of managing MRO operations is managing inventory, and the most important goal here is to reduce service inventories and support more stocking locations at a lower cost. Doing so can slash turnaround times and operating costs.

Configuration Control

Configuration management is a key AA&D challenge. For any aircraft, or other complex item, configuration information falls into two categories. The *master configuration* defines an item's assembly model—the part, alternative part(s), reference information, and assembly diagrams for all possible configurations of the item. For example, an aircraft with engine X requires fuel pump Y; if it is a cargo hauler, it requires landing gear assemblies of type M; if it is operated in cold climates, it requires kit F; etc. The serial number of part A must be tracked; part B must be replaced every 500 cycles or 2 years, and when it is replaced part D must also be replaced. The rules that govern these relationships are determined by the manufacturer, with additional requirements imposed by the operator and the FAA.

The current configuration of a specific unit is known as the *as-installed* or *unit configuration*. This configuration determines the specific maintenance requirements to ensure operational readiness. During maintenance, part information in the unit configuration is augmented, where applicable, to include inspection results, times and cycles, and individual part serial numbers. Unit configurations change continually.

The amount of configuration information represented by a fleet of aircraft is staggering. A relatively simple engine—such as an Allison 750-C20 turbine, with approximately 10,000 parts—has over 1200 valid configurations; the number of different as-installed configurations numbers in the thousands. A Boeing 777-300, by comparison, has over 3 million parts. As a rule, configurations are still tracked manually, using paper documentation. Most aircraft today cannot lift the documentation that defines their possible configurations.

Automating configuration management requires more than just collecting information in a database. Automation software must be able to interpret the rules and dependencies within a master configuration in order to create valid unit configurations or to verify imported unit information. Automating the master configuration enables such things as linking certified repair procedures to assemblies; the procedures would then become part of comprehensive and accurate maintenance plans for unit configurations. An electronic unit configuration—tied to a master configuration and containing time, cycle, and maintenance information for each part and assembly—can enable instant access to the service readiness and maintenance status of any component.

Information Management

The primary MRO process is job execution, and the shop floor is the center of this activity. Maintenance procedures are more complex and dynamic than manufacturing procedures. The scope of work is often unknown until disassembly is under way, and shop-floor bottlenecks can further complicate procedures. MRO documentation includes aircraft maintenance manuals, illustrated parts catalogs, fault isolation manuals, maintenance tips, overhaul manuals, structural repair manuals, service bulletins, advisory circulars, and airworthiness directives (ADs). The FAA uses ADs to communicate technical maintenance information, which often requires immediate compliance by maintenance organizations; adherence to such directives can have critical safety and legal ramifications.

Given that the technical information used to guide MRO operations must be complete, accurate, and current, maintenance support documents must be carefully managed. Here the paper trail ascends a cellulose mountain. Roomsful of manuals are moved manually, maintained with archaic processes (remember change pages? — they're still with us), and consulted with time-honored tediousness. Putting these mountains online is part of the answer, but the full solution lies in creating an information system in which part and assembly data are intelligently linked to maintenance requirements and workflow, and in which the MRO information is tied into related back-office systems. Steps are being taken in this direction. Systems now exist in which, for example, inputting an airworthiness directive can launch a workflow to ensure that a maintenance engineering committee convenes to discuss a compliance strategy for the AD.

In preventive maintenance in general, and aviation MRO in particular, the term *route* or *work card* refers to a maintenance procedure. Route management consists of developing and maintaining validated service procedures and optimizing their execution. Considerations in generating optimal routes include knowing the availabilities of spare parts, special tools, materials (e.g., sheet aluminum for airframe repairs), and required expertise. For instance, workers need to be aware of the schedules of authorized inspectors.

In many paper-based operations, work cards are printed on 4×6 cards. If a maintenance technician requires additional information to complete a task, a manual or manuals must be consulted. Time-and-motion studies of aircraft maintenance have shown that technicians can spend as much as 40 percent of their time walking back and forth between the aircraft and the manuals. This time represents a considerable expense, because an aircraft's maintenance visit may consist of hundreds of tasks: a typical annual check, commonly known as a

C check, can require over 2000 person-hours to complete. Arch supports alone could probably help the bottom line, but of course the real answer is automation. Advances in route management include bringing information and applications to the technician, in the form of wireless, wearable terminals that provide work-order specifics, maintenance tasks with all necessary documentation, and the ability to launch workflows (e.g., to notify an inspector when a job is complete).

Plan the Work, Work the Plan

A maintenance requirement contains four major sections; these specify the origin of the requirement, its effectivity (the units to which it applies), its frequency, and its work requirements. The key considerations for the planning, execution, and tracking of maintenance requirements include regulatory compliance, cost-effectiveness, and resource availability.

A maintenance planner may need to interpret what the originating document says regarding effectivity in order to track the requirements to the affected units. Sometimes effectivity is based simply on part number and/or serial number; in more complex cases, effectivity may be based on utilization, configuration, modification status, sampling algorithm, and current condition. To cover all effectivity possibilities, planning software must be able to model the effectivity of a maintenance requirement using the product classification and master and unit configurations in conjunction with a fleet-level maintenance program.

Performing a maintenance task later than indicated by the predefined frequency is a violation of regulations; performing the task too early is not cost-effective. A challenge of efficient maintenance planning is optimizing the task schedule, taking into consideration the frequency, maintenance opportunity, and resource availability. Maintenance-planning software must be able to provide views of all the maintenance requirements that apply to a unit, the time remaining for each requirement, and the service level (difficulty) of the requirements, thus enabling a planner to schedule the tasks during the appropriate maintenance visits.

To ensure smooth execution at maintenance facilities, long-, medium-, and short-term plans must be constantly updated to cope with business needs. Long-term planning requires software that models maintenance events and resource requirements and performs what-if analyses for scenarios such as fleet growth and increases in maintenance due to fleet aging. For maintenance-visit (medium-term) planning, software should enable a planner to define the work scope; to compile the corresponding labor, tool, and material requirements; and to create the jobs to be performed during a visit. Production-planning modules serve to manage the short-term task assignment and resource allocation for a maintenance visit. Production data such as the area of an aircraft being worked on, task sequence, and technician expertise are grouped and scheduled to optimize production. Shop-floor software must roll up labor costs, maintain job status, and serve to record repair data for critical parts and assemblies.

This maintenance knowledge base for each unit will help solve a major problem in maintenance planning: the inability to accurately forecast repair needs, including the corresponding labor and material requirements. A major challenge in the highly regulated maintenance industry is to create, maintain, and provide access to "cradle-to-grave" maintenance information for tracked components. For parts with tracking requirements, maintenance data need to be recorded in the unit configuration.

The Right Technology

The problems presented by the MRO industry are best met with applications that address industry-specific needs and also integrate with the back-office functionality required by any business. The full range of MRO processes should be automated and integrated— including scheduled and nonroutine maintenance, parts and component repair, job scheduling and routing, service bulletin management, fleet management, contract administration and monitoring, parts distribution, and billing. A solution would automate such tasks as parts verification, creating and modifying repair routes, and scheduling repair procedures.

Back-office areas that need special attention to meet the needs of businesses that perform advanced service include bills of material, contracts, costing, inventory, order entry, purchasing, shipping, receiving, and workflow. The activities of the shop floor are reflected in inventory, labor, and cost transactions. All costs associated with jobs should be collected throughout the repair cycle and automatically sent to integrated financial applications. Contract information should be available to applications that need it and to subcontractors and sister organizations. Examples include permissions for rotable inventories, configuration changes, scrap approvals, approval levels, and minimum build goals.

Competition among service providers amplifies the need to recognize and analyze trends quickly and to make informed, accurate decisions. To do this, it is critical to have an information management foundation that ties together all aspects of the enterprise. Reducing the complexity of the service enterprise and increasing its responsiveness is essential. Diverse functions must be integrated, and the integrated system must be administered from a central site and available to all maintenance facilities worldwide.

At the heart of aviation and defense is complexity—in the configurations, the inventory requirements, the maintenance requirements, and the procedures for performing maintenance. Simplification is at the heart of the solution—integrated applications that support the flow of data through the service enterprise. The logistics of servicing a fleet of aircraft are considerable, the amounts of information and data mountainous. The solution is not to move the mountain but to put it online, use automation to minimize the stumbling blocks, and make the results globally available. Operating costs will be reduced and efficiency enhanced, without compromising safety.

Consumer Packaged Goods

Introduction

Consumer packaged goods (CPG) is a huge industry, generating revenues of some $500 billion per year. By convention, it comprises five segments: alcoholic beverages, food and nonalcoholic beverages, household nondurables, over-the-counter pharmaceuticals, and tobacco. Each of the top 100 CPG companies generates revenues of more than $2 billion, while another 900 generate $100 million to $2 billion each. This huge industry has a huge problem.

To generate that $500 billion, the industry incurs $265 billion in cost of goods sold (COGS), the largest expense category for this industry. This figure can be reduced in ways enabled by software; but this is true of most industries and is in no way specific to CPG. Instead we focus here on promotion, which accounts for $135 billion in annual expenses, more than a quarter of total revenues. This figure is the sum of $35 billion in advertising, $65 billion in trade promotions, and $35 billion in promotions of other types.

Trade Promotions

CPG manufacturers can control their advertising expenses just as businesses in other industries can. The distinctive expense in this industry is trade promotions, which pose an enormous difficulty for the manufacturers and an enormous challenge for software developers. Trade promotions comprise discounts to retailers, which the retailers may pass on in any degree to consumers, and temporary price reductions (TPRs), which the retailers are obliged to pass on. In return for a promotion of either kind, the manufacturer may require a reciprocal effort by the retailer—for instance, preferential display of the manufacturer's products.

The Problem: Complexity

Trade promotions is an area of daunting complexity. Whereas special offers from car manufacturers or financial companies are typically uniform nationwide, trade promotions in CPG are normally regional (at most) and may need to change rapidly to reflect the relative success in local or regional markets of one or more of the manufacturer's products. A manufacturer might offer a TPR to boost sales of corn flakes in San Diego, where they are flagging; at the same time, corn flakes might be flying off the shelves in Los Angeles at the expense of oatmeal, which needs special terms to compete effectively there.

CPG corporate executives can allocate funds for promotions that apply to all retailers in one category or another, but the need for sensitivity and rapid response in local and regional sales situations means that a large proportion of promotional funds is put under the control of brokers and sales reps whose job it is to deal directly with the retailers. An average sales rep who is authorized to cut deals totaling up to a given amount will often exceed that amount, and the deals that the rep agrees to are often recorded inadequately, if at all.

Because CPG retailers typically survive on razor-thin margins, their practice is to deduct the nominal amount of the deal from the amount they pay the manufacturer for the goods to be sold; thus it becomes the manufacturer's problem to reconcile its accounts, to justify payments that fall short of the amounts invoiced, and to monitor retailers' compliance with their reciprocal commitments.

Promotional deductions, which totaled some $10 billion in 1999, are crucial in the industry, contributing about half of retailers' cumulative profits. But faulty and inadequate recording of these deductions means major losses for manufacturers. Receipt of a short payment usually means a manual hunt for an explanation, which is a serious administrative expense; worse, the hunt currently fails about 14 percent of the time, meaning that some $1.4 billion annually in manufacturers' expenses is simply written off. Further, inadequate records mean that manufacturers must forgo vital business intelligence: promotions, after all, are designed to boost sales, and reliable advance warning of which products are going to sell faster would allow manufacturers more detailed control of supply chains and inventories, enabling them not only to save money on storage and spoilage but also to exploit opportunities for enhanced sales.

The Software Challenge

The central challenge here for software vendors is the complexity of the process, which poses severe demands for data entry, data storage, and data organization. Once the needed data are captured, the process calls for tight integration between CRM and ERP applications: programs for marketing, sales, and pricing on the CRM side must coordinate effectively with ERP systems for order management, accounts payable and receivable, and general ledger. Partner relationship management (PRM) software is needed as well, and there is an obvious requirement for mobile applications that can synchronize field operations with central corporate data repositories.

This area of applications is called *trade management*, and its potential for business intelligence is leading the industry to *collaborative planning for forecasting and replenishment* (CPFR), which promises sweeping advances in the production and delivery of goods. The scope and complexity of the applications needed make this area an ideal target for a comprehensive suite of e-business software.

Financial Services
Introduction

The global financial services industry has changed tremendously over the last few years. While business goals remain the same—*manage performance, improve efficiencies, retain profitable customers*, and *expand markets*—massive change is being driven by

- Changing regulations
- Ongoing industry consolidation
- Broadening of product lines
- The changing role of field agents
- Problems posed by disparate legacy and proprietary systems
- The growing development of alternative channels, including call centers and the Web
- The need to provide each employee with a 360º view of the customer, in part to promote customer retention

Changing Regulations

Many countries around the world are allowing the market a freer hand in financial services. They are implementing regulations to encourage competition between financial service companies while opening their markets to foreign companies. In the United States, the Gramm-Leach-Bliley Act, which President Clinton signed into law in late 1999, eliminated Depression-era laws and regulations that strictly separated the activities of U.S. banks, securities firms, and insurers. The resultant blurring of differences among financial service providers, while new to the United States, has been a fact of life in many other countries for some time. To compete in the U.S. market, financial service companies will need to deliver consistent product information while satisfying the commissioners and regulators of as many as 50 different states.

Industry Consolidation

Ongoing industry consolidation will continue to exert a major influence on the success of CRM implementations. Merging financial institutions will need to

- Reconcile different corporate cultures, resolving intercompany hostilities and negative perceptions
- Standardize global sales and service practices
- Resolve which operational systems will be retained and/or consolidated
- Consolidate such systems accordingly, then arrange for appropriate distribution, both internally and externally, of the information they generate
- Retrain corporate staffs to meet redefined objectives
- Navigate the world of cross-selling and up-selling

Broadening of Product Lines

Financial service companies have traditionally been product-oriented. Banks have generally offered a variety of products and services. The typical insurance company, by contrast, has restricted itself to a narrow product line; its information systems, Web site(s), call centers, and other channels generally reflect this narrow orientation. The challenge for such companies is to integrate many disparate product-accounting systems, then to distribute the information these systems generate across a large number of channels to improve customer service and to increase selling opportunities. Currently, a customer who calls into a call center for one line of business (LOB) to request information on an account belonging to a different LOB will often be transferred to a different agent and may even have to call a different number.

The Changing Role of Field Agents

Field agents constitute an expensive distribution channel, and the growth of call centers has brought their cost-effectiveness into question. Their future role will be largely confined to promoting complex products that require direct personal contact and significant documentation. The banking industry is implementing specific programs that direct field agents to target the banks' preferred and profitable customers in order to improve sales and customer retention. Field agents need complete and current customer information to perform sales and service transactions while integrating their work, as appropriate, with other distribution channels.

Legacy and Proprietary Systems

Because software vendors were slow to develop financial services systems, companies in the industry developed a variety of highly customized proprietary systems. Recent merger and acquisition activity, coupled with new demand for CRM solutions, has compelled the companies involved to try to reconcile often incompatible systems, heightening the complexity of developing a common 360º view of the customer. For example, a banking customer might have a checking account, a savings account, a line of credit, a credit card, a mortgage, a leased vehicle, and one or more investments. Within many banks, the accounting information for each product line resides on its own legacy system.

Alternative Channels: Call Centers and the Web

To reduce operational costs, financial service companies are trying to divert transactions from bank tellers and platform personnel to more cost-effective channels, notably call centers and the Web. These are efficient for four main reasons:

- By selling directly to the consumer, these channels obviate paying commissions or other fees to intermediaries such as insurance agents or bank customer service representatives (CSRs).

- By centralizing operations, they achieve higher productivity and economies of scale.

- The Web is effectively present everywhere. Call centers, meanwhile, can be located in places that are less costly than the headquarters cities of financial service companies.

- These channels can exploit technology that enables more rapid and thorough responses to inquiries than can be provided by a teller at a bank window.

Customers are demanding unlimited access to their financial service providers, regardless of time, channel, or location. Call centers and the Web are becoming the preferred means of providing such access because they extend both the hours and the reach of those providers. With the Interstate Banking and Branching Act of 1994 having eliminated geographical constraints, financial service companies can establish themselves anywhere; but the only effective way for them to cover their newly expanded territories is through the call center or the Web.

Know Your Customer

Because acquiring customers is very expensive, customer retention is crucial to the success of any financial services company. Companies lose money on short-term customers and only break even after about two years; to realize a profit, they must retain customers longer and expand their current relationships with customers who are potentially, but not yet actually, profitable.

A financial company can succeed only by showing that it understands its customer's needs. To do so, it requires comprehensive and consistent information about each customer. Ideally, this will reside in a central customer profile that records the history of the customer's interactions with the company, shows what products and services the customer is using, and provides a basis for projections as to additional products and services that the customer might want. Whenever the customer contacts a company representative, the rep needs ready access to the profile to ensure that the company provides the best possible customer service.

The Future

Financial service companies must be able to deliver a variety of complex products and services to a variety of discriminating customers, ensuring convenience, comfort, and care. The services must also be available over a variety of channels—call center, Internet, branch—with fast, personalized service from qualified employees. Companies must accomplish all this while continuing to manage risk effectively and to enhance company profits.

Figure 7-1[3] forecasts that revenues from packaged CRM software for the financial services industry in North America will triple between 1999 and 2004, starting from $547 million and reaching $1.8 billion by 2004 year-end. To accomplish this goal, successful CRM solutions for financial services companies must support seamless

---

[3]Figure 7-1 is drawn from International Data Corporation study #24057, dated March 2001.

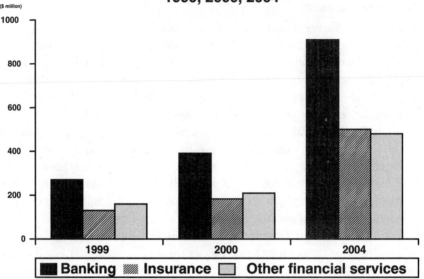

Figure 7-1. Packaged-Software Revenues for Finance Sector, Observed and Predicted

exchange of information among all related applications, to ensure constant updating and refinement of CRM processes. If a customer uses a PC-banking connection to report a changed phone number, the number must be updated in the data warehouse so that a call-center campaign running the next day will not call the wrong number. An integrated solution must support

- Access to operational and analytical customer data
- Applications to underpin customer-related decisions (customer-profitability analysis, data mining, database marketing, and campaign management)
- Integrated, individualized interactions that provide a full 360º view of the customer

Access to Customer Data

Since 1977, financial service companies have spent more than $175 billion on technology infrastructure. A significant portion of this spending was on back-end legacy systems.

Operational Data

For every customer, a financial institution needs to gather and organize the *operational* data—data regarding specific interactions between the institution and the customer. This process, which is essential for service, also provides strong support for sales initiatives. The need to retain profitable customers will drive financial service institutions to support multiple business functions, products, and lines of business in an integrated environment, enabling the coordination of operational data that will provide a true 360º customer view both to the customer and to customer-facing employees. Timely, complete, and accurate information will enable employees to execute "once and done" service and sales.

Analytical Data

Developing and maintaining *analytical* customer-level data has traditionally been difficult and/or expensive for many financial institutions, but this problem was largely solved in the 1990s with the advent of customer data warehouses (or data marts). First and foremost, a data warehouse serves to provide a model for deeper understanding of the behavior and needs of customers—and to relate this understanding to the financial service institution's objectives. Achieving excellence in customer service is increasingly difficult without a customer data warehouse as a source of critical information for operational systems.

Applications to Support Customer-Related Decisions

A complete CRM solution that integrates analytical and operational information will include sets of decision-support applications.

Customer-Profitability Analysis

These applications are designed to identify effective mixes of revenue opportunities and cost-effective channels for attracting and serving customers profitably. Leading institutions continue to advance their sophistication in measuring customer profitability. An important branch of this research is capacity-utilization cost modeling.

Data Mining

Data mining means using automated or semiautomated applications to analyze large data sets to discover and confirm meaningful patterns.

Predicting and scoring future customer behavior are popular uses of these applications. Data-mining solutions are integral to database marketing initiatives.

Database Marketing

Database marketing focuses on identifying products that are of value to specific prospects. The use of analytical tools to segment lists of prospects and customers and to coordinate internal and third-party data can provide a reliable basis for targeted marketing.

Campaign Management

Financial service institutions are becoming more sophisticated as they move from list pulling through database marketing toward enterprise customer management. Campaign-management applications help to manage complex segment-selection criteria, to track customer responses, to assess tactical efficiency, and to provide decision-scoring analytics.

Integrated, Individualized Interactions

The growth of technology—and experiences with Amazon.com and other leading retailers—is changing customer expectations. The customer typically targeted by financial service companies now expects a fully integrated, individualized interaction, whether the customer is visiting the company in person, over the telephone, or on the Internet. Financial service companies expect their CRM solutions to accommodate industry-specific needs ranging from the user interface to the business functionality required to sell to and serve their customers.

Integrated Relationship Access

Integrated relationship access means that all customer-contact channels are sharing information with one another in real time, making it possible for any customer to see consistent views of his or her relationship with the financial institution—regardless of when, where, or how contact is made. Such integration also enables the institution to deal consistently—often by automated means—with the customer, regardless of the channel being used. Applications enabling this ideal could include workflow packages coupled with a data store common to all channels.

Distributed, Individualized Marketing Interactions

Distributed, individualized marketing interactions are rapidly emerging. Several key components must converge to provide the leverage needed at the point of customer contact; these include customer-specific knowledge, selling skills appropriate to the development of one-to-one relationships, and the ability to measure individual marketing performance.

Government

United States governments, at all levels, are businesses. Many of them are transforming themselves into e-businesses at various rates, and the others will experience intense pressure from their constituents to do so. Like private enterprises, governments will find that by moving their activities online, they can simultaneously achieve tremendous economies and improve service to their customers—in this case, American citizens.

Although this section holds many implications for state and local governments, it will focus on the federal government, for which the Internet poses several challenges:

1. To make e-government a priority
2. To reengineer the channels by which the government provides information and services to its citizens
3. To promote American economic expansion by guaranteeing universal Web access to a fully connected citizenry

Government differs from private enterprise in that it is less driven by competition. While there is clearly some room for competitive pressures among state and local governments, there is virtually none for the federal government, which can hardly be said to compete (for instance) with the governments of Canada and Mexico. Instead, the U.S. government will be pulled into e-business by the lure of increased efficiencies and of the enormous savings these efficiencies will generate, and it will be pushed by its citizens, who—once they experience the benefits of an e-government that is accessible at all times—will clamor for additional government services to be Web-enabled.

The absence of competition is an advantage of sorts for government. But it faces two problems that set it apart from all other industries. The first is that its "customer set" includes millions of people who cannot afford to pay for the government services they need. The second is that "government" (in reality, multiple overlapping governments at multiple levels) is tremendously massive and complex; for this reason, the difficulty of organizing e-government exceeds, by degrees of magnitude, that of organizing any business.

E-Citizenship

However great the advantages to be gained by the government's *internal* transformation into an e-business, those to be gained by wiring its citizenry are potentially stunning. First, of course, everybody would be linked electronically to everybody else; if you wanted to communicate with your cousin in Ketchikan, you could do so at once, regardless of time differences, and at no cost. (Of course your cousin might have moved to Ketchikan to get away from you, but there are some problems that even the Internet can't solve.) This would also be true for people who wanted to communicate with businesses, which of course would mean all sizable businesses abroad as well as those in the United States.

Moreover, everybody would be able to communicate directly with the government itself. No more listening through eighty-three rings of the phone or four identical renditions of *Rhapsody in Blue*; no more waiting for a convenient time to call during limited government office hours; no more having to deal with a human being when you only need to fill out a form; no more getting misdirected, or endlessly redirected, by human beings you speak to.

Among the services that the government could implement across the Web are many relating to the filing and payment of federal taxes, which could be implemented in large part for everybody and in full for the great majority. The provision of a set of displayable forms that would automate simple data checking, arithmetic, and item copying would be an invaluable service; many taxpayers would be able to submit their returns without ever handling paper forms. The IRS could use the Internet to send an e-mail acknowledging the receipt of each tax return, and to provide audit status and refunds. Fewer federal employees could process the nation's returns in less time than before, saving money for the taxpayer and generating earlier refunds. The Internet tax system should also be designed to encourage efforts by private enterprise to provide additional filing services.

Other potential services involve voter registration and voting. By extending Internet access as broadly as possible, and by enabling its citizens to vote using the Net, the government could very vigorously increase the rate of participation in the political process. In the Democratic primary election in Arizona in the year 2000, more than 35,000 votes were cast online, while participation increased almost threefold compared to the 1996 primary. Internet voting is almost certain to spread, especially now that the government has set standards for digital signatures, which are most likely to be used as reliable identification.

E-government would also enable citizens to use the Internet to apply for and be issued permits and licenses. Now that businesses can use www.e-stamp.com to print postage off the Internet, there is no reason why driver's licenses and registrations, building permits, and hunting and fishing permits should not be available electronically. Again, providing such services over the Internet would not *cost* money, it would *save* money, and it would enhance constituent satisfaction, by allowing citizens to serve themselves. The goal is to get them online—and out of lines.

Yet the benefits of e-citizenship extend far beyond direct government services. The value of universal access to information is immeasurable. Health care would be improved if doctors could access *all* relevant information about their patients, and if patients could access information about their maladies. Education could be advanced by eliminating geographical distance, bringing the finest instruction to every home, school, library, and community. The benefits of using the Web are such that it is likely to boost literacy. Electronic shopping, chat, and streaming audio and video can connect the elderly, who too often live out their later years in isolation.

The Digital Divide

According to the U.S. Census Bureau, there are currently about 104 million American households. Judging by figures from the

Department of Commerce (DoC),[4] 51 percent of these have computers, and 43 percent have access to the Internet; about 46 percent of all individuals are actually using the Internet.

There has been a great deal of hand-wringing ·over the Digital Divide, the statistical gap in access between some more-privileged or more-attuned segments of the population and others less so. Early concern that women were using the Internet less than men has evaporated recently with the publication of studies showing that gender has scarcely any bearing on access rates.

On the other hand, some minority groups are clearly lagging; for example, according to the same DoC report, black and Hispanic households in the United States have access to the Internet at only 57 percent of the general rate. (Yet access for both groups is growing faster than that for the general population.) Persons with disabilities have access to the Net at only half the rate of those without disabilities. In mid-1999, 7.5 percent of all Americans lived in areas that still had no Internet service.

The federal government has long recognized the importance of universal service as an engine of social cohesion; this is why it costs you the same amount to send a first-class letter to Anchorage or to Presque Isle as it does to send one to your neighbor.[5] This principle was further promoted by the Telecommunications Act of 1996, which included an "e-rate" program providing for discounted Internet access for the nation's schools and libraries. In consequence, more than 95 percent of American schools are now online. This program demonstrates that federal initiatives for the Internet can succeed; the government now needs to ask itself why, in the information age, children need the Internet but low-income adults do not.

Step 1: Making E-Government a Priority

Because the scope of the federal government's self-conversion into an e-business is formidable, such a conversion calls for the creation

---

[4] *Falling Through the Net: Toward Digital Inclusion*, October 2000.

[5] In fact, the history of the USPS, and of the U.S. Post Office before it, is a record of success based on reliability and technical innovation. It demonstrates that the federal government can rise effectively to the challenge of establishing and maintaining connections among Americans.

of a federal technology authority. This need is recognized by the Electronic Government Act of 2001, which would establish a federal CIO in the Office of Management and Budget. It would be the CIO's responsibility to promote e-government and to implement governmental information policy. The CIO would oversee not merely the initial conversion but the ongoing maintenance, development, and optimization of electronic government.

The first challenge for e-government is to centralize and to rationalize the federal information services. Oracle once had thousands of computers and thousands of IT staff, in hundreds of locations, performing tasks that at best were duplicative and at worst were mutually incompatible; the government *still* has such inefficiencies, but on a much larger scale. When redundant tasks are eliminated and the surviving tasks are rationalized, as Oracle has done, the savings are awe-inspiring. In Washington's case, they would probably amount to tens of billions of dollars per year. And the almost inescapable side effect would be improved service to the government's citizens, service that is not only less expensive but also more rapid, more reliable, and more consistent.

The federal program would be responsible not only for coordinating the countless departments and agencies within the federal government, but also for meshing all efforts at the federal level with e-government initiatives by state and local governments. This is the only way to provide citizens with a single comprehensive portal through which to interact with their government as a whole.

Step 2: The Federal Portal

In June 2000, President Clinton announced the implementation of FirstGov.gov, a single point through which citizens can access federal Web sites and information services. This portal facilitates access to almost all federal sites.

FirstGov.gov is an important first step. But it falls short of what is needed, largely because it does not take advantage of what has been learned over the last five years about Web-site design, navigation, and function. FirstGov.gov is a 20th-century portal trying to meet 21st-century needs.

First, the portal does not support personalization. The United States has 275 million people; their needs and interests in relation to government are more various and complex than government itself. What they need is MyFirstGov.gov, which could be customized by every user to suit his or her distinct concerns.

Second, the portal must be extended to embrace state and local governments. Citizens often do not know which level of government to turn to; they may try in vain to find services at one level that are actually available at another level. And they should not need to learn one or more new governmental URLs whenever they move five miles. The goal is to provide them with a uniform view of all government.

Third, FirstGov.gov is hopelessly complex. Searches I tried on "Social Security," "Medicare," and "IRS" yielded 187,980 hits, 57,310 hits, and 72,390 hits, respectively, and these numbers may be expected to grow. Even the most experienced Web surfer would be overwhelmed by such results. Federal Webmasters could turn to Amazon or Yahoo! to learn how to harness what is potentially the greatest asset of the Web: simplicity. For one thing, every search facility could be provided with an option to constrain its search to the current page and all pages logically subordinate to it.

(The numbers of hits returned by searches are swollen by multiple appearances of virtually every document, a fact that reflects another problem. Unless the government works hard to minimize duplicates, every update to a document will threaten to leave multiple copies that are in conflict one with another, and every time an out-of-date document is deleted its doppelgängers may survive to spread confusion.)

Fourth, the government needs to implement a uniform look and feel across all its Web sites. No matter how reliably any federal site conforms to its *own* standards, finding two sites that look alike is almost impossible. Given that people already find it confusing to deal with government, the various sites need to be made to conform to a standard look and feel, so that experience gained by users of any one site can help them in dealing with others.

Fifth, users need to interact with the government, not just read about it. Far too many federal sites make it easy to study the history of an agency or the biography of its chief, but provide little or no practical service. Agencies must ask themselves how people need to interact with them and then make it easy for people to do so. Services and forms relevant to people's most frequent needs must be presented front and center. This will serve not only the users of the sites but the agencies themselves, which will find their workloads reduced and much of their paperwork eliminated.

The list of services that the federal portal might span is endless. I can only begin to suggest its breadth:

- A hierarchical view of federal departments, branches, and agencies
- A sophisticated search engine spanning the entire site
- An indexed listing of job openings
- Forms of all kinds
- A list of bills pending in Congress
- A calendar of events related to or sponsored by government
- Recommendations for citizen participation in government
- Postal services, including rate tables and facilities for purchasing stamps, for paying bills, and for buying special supplies or collectibles
- Gift shops for various departments (e.g., the Department of the Treasury)
- www.whitehouse.gov, www.senate.gov, and www.house.gov
- Applications for Temporary Assistance for Needy Families and for Aid to Families with Dependent Children
- U.S. Supreme Court decisions and the Court's calendar
- Social Security System information, including histories of past and projections of future payments
- Department of Education resources, including presentations of types of education loans available and methods for applying for loans
- Web cameras: for Congress, for the Bureau of Engraving and Printing, etc.

Many of these services, and many others as well, are already available across the Web. The challenge is to continuously augment and coordinate the services available until anybody with Internet access can easily find, through the federal portal, virtually any service that might reasonably be sought there.

Step 3: Universal Access

The federal government can serve its constituents by initiating a National Internet Access Program (NIAP). The point of the program would be not to demonstrate our superiority to the Russians or to invent such things as Styrofoam but to bring Americans into an ever closer union, not only with one another but with the rest of the world—with its diversity of cultures and its infinite resources of knowledge, information, and goods.

The NIAP would be a two-part program designed to erase the digital divide. The first part would establish an online exchange for used PCs and network computers. A tax deduction would be granted to anyone who donated to the exchange a device that could reasonably be used to access the Internet. Any device donated would then have to be certified as "Internet-ready," meaning that it would be equipped, as necessary, with an Internet browser and appropriate free plug-ins. It would then be issued to a qualified applicant.

The second part of the program would provide a $350 income-tax credit to cover purchase and maintenance costs (and Internet access fees, if any) for the first Internet-access device in each household. This amount would be fully adequate to cover the purchase of a network computer, if not that of a traditional PC.[6] This provision would be limited to households earning less than the median national income; consequently, poorer states would have higher proportions of eligible applicants.

If all qualifying American households that lack access were to take advantage of this program in its first year, the cost for that year would be no more than about $20 billion. In later years the cost would fall dramatically as more and more households came to own Internet-accessing devices. And the government could administer this program directly over the Internet, providing forms to be completed and submitted online.

Some would portray such a program as subsidizing the poor at the expense of those who are already "connected." In fact, the program

---

[6]Systems that are currently purchasable over the Internet for $330 include an Internet computer, a keyboard, a mouse, a 15-inch SVGA monitor, and speakers. As for Internet access, it is increasingly available for free; I expect that no-charge access will become the norm, with Internet service providers (ISPs) recouping their costs by selling advertising capacity—like today's television networks.

would bring major benefits for everybody; this is suggested by Metcalfe's Law, according to which the value of being connected to a network increases exponentially as the number of others connected increases. Beyond the simple value of an increased ability to communicate, the program would help to drive American commerce.

The program might also stipulate payments to individual states in order to encourage them to promote the Internet infrastructure they would need in order to approach 100 percent access. Because much of the needed infrastructure is already in place, these payments would be small by comparison with the reimbursements just proposed. They might sensibly be made proportional to each state's area divided by its population; legislators from the more populous states could be brought to see that universal access serves principles of fairness and unity whose value far surpasses a few billion dollars. And every state would perceive that it had much to gain by bringing its citizens online.

There are major precedents for a program of this sort. In February 2000, Ford Motor Company announced that it would offer every one of its 350,000 employees, for $5 per month, a home PC, an inkjet printer, and Internet access. Ford said that the offer was designed to keep its workers at the leading edge of e-business skills and technology. Delta Airlines quickly followed suit, announcing its own offer of a PC and Internet access to each of *its* 72,000 employees for $12 per month. Once more, American private enterprise has a lesson to teach the U.S. government.

National Commerce

Beyond all the services previously listed, there is a compelling reason for our government to move decisively to extend Internet access as widely as possible. This is that doing so will be good for business. It will stimulate growth in e-commerce and help all the companies that deal with their customers directly across the Web. It will promote the growth of Internet infrastructure providers. It will make it easier for would-be consumers to find and purchase the goods they want, in part because the efficiencies offered by e-business will lower—or at least hold down—purchase prices. The Internet is already contributing strongly to the national economy. By acting to extend and to strengthen the influence of the Internet, the government can leverage its enormous influence to enhance the impact of the Net and to spread its benefits even to the least privileged among us.

Government can do much more than merely enable Internet commerce; it can drive it. According to a study released in late May 2001,[7] the U.S. federal government is already the largest online retailer in America (in the world?); its annual dollar volume of $3.6 billion surpasses that of Amazon, at $2.8 billion. However, $3.3 billion of the federal total is derived from online sales of savings bonds and treasury bills and notes. What's more, the federal effort spans more than 160 distinct sites; it has no comprehensive organization, and most of the sites require some additional offline effort by would-be purchasers. There is immeasurable room for improving services to citizens, not only by enabling them to save money and trouble through online transactions, but also by reducing government expenses in moving goods, thus reducing the burden that government imposes on taxpayers.

Government can also use the Internet for its purchases. According to a report released by Jupiter Media Metrix on May 30, 2001, only 1 percent of federal spending during 2000 took place over the Net. Although the report projects that this figure will rise to 17 percent (about $285 billion) by 2005, governmental e-procurement is hobbled by the lack of standards for transactions. Addressing this problem could enable governments at all levels to exploit the Net much more effectively and, in so doing, to improve their own operating efficiency and the general health of American business.

Conclusion

A full-throttle effort to move the federal government onto the Internet would give new and dramatic meaning to the phrase *reinventing government*. But such an effort must be reciprocated by moving American citizens onto the Net as well. This twofold enterprise would strengthen our sense of national unity, would make it easier and more pleasant for citizens to deal with their government, and would promote commerce and the economy as a whole.

---

[7]"Dot-gov goes retail," *Federal Computer Week*, May 28, 2001. See http://www.fcw.com/fcw/articles/2001/0528/cov-main-05-28-01.asp.

However, even if doing all this will pay for itself many times over in the long run, it will still require initial funding and consequently will have to contend with all the other claims on the federal purse. It will not happen, and it will never get an opportunity to enrich all our lives, if it is not sponsored by a leader with the courage, conviction, and authority to carry it to fruition. In the 1960s we had leaders with the will to drive Old Glory to the moon. It is not too much, in the new millennium, to ask for the leadership needed to accomplish a project that, while much less daunting technically, promises far more practical value than Project Apollo ever delivered. It will also be far less expensive: going to the moon cost us about $20 billion in 1967/68 dollars; translated into year-2000 currency, that's more than $100 billion.

Leasing

Overview

Equipment leasing is big business. There are more than 2,000 equipment-leasing companies in the United States alone, where 31 percent of the $593 billion of equipment acquired in 1998 was leased. The Equipment Leasing Association (ELA) categorizes equipment lessors as independent, captive, and bank lessors. Independent lessors are typically finance companies that are not affiliated with any particular manufacturer or dealer that offer leases directly to businesses. Captive leasing companies are financial subsidiaries of dealers or manufacturing companies, and bank lessors are the leasing subsidiaries or divisions of banks.

Equipment leasing is big business because it is attractive to both lessors and lessees. In the United States, 80 percent of businesses have at least one lease. Lease financing provides lessors great flexibility in their equipment purchases, cash management, and financial planning. Lessees gain a number of business benefits; they can

- Take advantage of flexible financing options
- Manage their cash flow effectively, matching rental payments to revenues earned from assets
- Use off-balance-sheet leases in order to retain borrowing capacity needed for working capital

- Improve operating efficiency by focusing on core business concerns instead of asset management

- Outsource to lessors the acquisition, maintenance, and disposition of equipment

- Reduce exposure to technological obsolescence

- Avoid other risks of ownership

Challenges

Profitability

The leasing industry must revise its traditional strategies in order to address the opportunities and threats created by new technology. Challenges are posed by the proliferation of efficient delivery channels, a tight labor market, corporate consolidation, restricted funding sources, and general economic uncertainty. Industry executives and managers need to maneuver through an increasingly competitive and volatile business environment to increase market share while remaining profitable.

Maintaining strong customer relationships and attracting new customers are extremely important in equipment leasing. Lessors that expand their marketing channels to access new prospects and to provide customers with the greatest added value will win. Bank and captive lessors have a competitive advantage because their parent companies have existing customer relationships and/or involve the leasing subsidiary in the original equipment sale.

Productivity and reduced operating costs are also important. Lessors that can cut costs or allocate operating expenses to the parent company can increase their profits. Here again, captive and bank lessors enjoy a competitive advantage because they share the costs of operations, lease origination, and contract administration with their parent companies.

Old and Rich Systems

Leasing companies face additional internal challenges with their business process and legacy systems. Many legacy systems in the industry were originally "best of breed" solutions; although functionally rich, they are fragmented and ingrown and use obsolete architectures. The typical system is a web of custom interfaces gluing together multiple point solutions that have not been designed to work with one another; this patchwork approach results in serious integration problems and inflexibility. Its complexities are compounded when global leasing requirements—local customs and business processes, generally accepted accounting principles (GAAP) and tax regulations—are integrated. Aging systems and business processes cannot be readily upgraded, and, because they are incompatible with recent technology, they cannot fully exploit the opportunities offered by e-business.

Features vs. Business Processes

These problems of legacy systems are compounded by the leasing industry's traditional focus on improving system features rather than business processes. Unlike conventional manufacturing companies, equipment-leasing companies have not had to evolve their systems and business processes in order to remain competitive. Manufacturing companies have been compelled to improve their business processes continually, moving from MRP I to MRP II to just-in-time to advanced planning and other sophisticated manufacturing processes. Many manufacturing companies see e-business as one more evolutionary cycle; because equipment leasing has not experienced the same pressure to evolve, it now views e-business as a major revolution.

E-Business Competition

Established leasing companies now find themselves threatened by newcomers which, not being burdened by legacy systems and inefficient business processes, can easily implement e-business solutions to access their customers and provide fast responsive service. Most older companies have responded to this threat by adding Web-based front ends to their legacy systems. This is a stopgap: their legacy systems and business processes must still be improved to take full advantage of the power of e-business technology.

E-Business Strategies

Leasing-industry CEOs, management, and professional services and software vendors understand that e-business is essential to addressing these challenges effectively. However, most of them are unclear about their e-business strategies and the first steps to take.

For this reason, implementing effective e-business solutions may present a tougher challenge in leasing than in other industries.

An e-business model must be simple, complete, and integrated. It must integrate equipment leasing applications across the entire life cycle of the lease: sales and origination, lease/loan authoring and accounting, disbursement, billing, payments, asset tracking, collections, restructuring and termination negotiations, and asset remarketing. It must replace current systems of separately architected applications with a global enterprise data model that presents an intuitive user interface to a family of tightly integrated applications founded on one global, manageable, and reliably available database and data center.

Media

A teacher logs on to the Web site of a major publisher and searches the publisher's content database for properties that he can license, download, and assemble into a course on the evolution of rock music. He wants digital files from print, graphic, audio, and video sources. Another major publisher can't offer this service because it does not have a single database cataloging all the properties it owns, it does not have all of its marketable content available in digital form, and its business software cannot support the number or type of business transactions required.

An ad agency searches the digital assets of Megafilm Studios online for a film from which it can license a five-second clip for use in an advertising campaign. It plans to use the video clip in four TV spots and the audio portion in ten radio commercials. It finds a film, defines the clip it wants, concludes an agreement online, and receives the film clip and invoice electronically. The agency is one of hundreds of consumers currently creating similar online agreements for digital information. Megafilm is not as big or important as its name implies, but all its assets are available and generating revenue, including such things as *Household Commercials from the 50s, Volume 2*, which it assembled from content it bought inexpensively at an online auction.

Are these situations far-fetched? A little, but only because we're not there yet—we *are* headed in that direction. And they do highlight the salient features of the new global media market:

- Demand based on consumer pull instead of distributor push
- The need to manage digital assets at a new level of refinement
- The need to assign and manage intellectual property rights with greater speed and control

And let me state unequivocally that your business systems must be able to handle the increased demands that will be coming. This is not a problem that can be solved by throwing people at it; the answer is efficiency, not effort.

Advances in computer and information technology and the rise to prominence of the Internet have created a corresponding growth in the types and amount of electronic media that need to be managed. At the simplest level is the need to gain and retain access to one's media assets. At the other end of the spectrum, where additional profits lie, is the need to manage the buying and selling of digital assets at vastly increased volumes; think grains of sand, not mountains.

Media management in the Internet Age includes everything from content creation and the business-to-business exchange of these assets to their delivery to customers—at any location, at any time, on demand. This *any-place any-time when-I-want-it* aspect of media management is an interesting inversion of the old model. It's where the new opportunities are—and the new challenges. In the old model, media items (e.g., newspapers and magazines) were centrally produced in identical units and distributed individually. Or they were centrally produced and distributed to groups of people: for example, tens of thousands of people would go to several multitheater cineplexes to view a few movies, and maybe one film, and pay exorbitant prices for snacks. The new model has large numbers of people sitting in their homes at the same time, watching a cable broadcast, eating cost-effective snacks bought in bulk at warehouse stores. And personalized home pages allow people to create essentially unique online i-papers and e-zines.

Cable subscription services were the beginning of the customer-distributor inversion—people staying home and the media coming to them. Pay-per-view adds the complexity of having to handle additional agreements for the service, but the numbers are not huge. Existing infrastructures have been able to handle the increased load.

Beyond this is the new media market, where consumers define the content they want, when they want it, and on what platform, then negotiate an agreement, obtain their content, and are charged for it.

Digital Asset Management

Digitizing of old analog and hard-copy originals has already progressed significantly, driven by the dramatic growth of the Internet and its inherent capability to provide on-demand access to digital libraries of words, pictures, audio, and video. Furthermore, much media content is now being developed in digital formats, in anticipation of rapidly evolving distribution channels such as interactive digital TV, games platforms, mobile telephony, and handheld devices. These changes have made media asset management a critical ingredient of business success. This reformatting becomes especially challenging if one considers that the salable asset may not actually exist until a consumer requests it—for example, it might comprise an online article consisting of prose, a copyrighted photo of a bird, and an audio clip of the bird's song, each with its own cost and license requirements that must be combined into a new contractual unit. How do you store, retrieve, and package your media assets so that such sales are possible?

Business Rights Management

Rights management is the second key to unlocking the possibilities. This can be done successfully only by automating the creation and tracking of the intellectual property rights and agreements that define and protect the use of a media asset. Companies must be able to buy and sell these rights and assign them to other companies or individuals as parts of business transactions. They must be able to negotiate contracts, process renewals, and track royalties. The contract management system should be able to do such things as notify a rights holder that a right is about to expire, provide an alert that (for example) distribution in a certain area is prohibited by contract, and report any disparity between rights and revenue. This information must feed easily into back-end systems such as invoicing and accounts receivable. And all of this must happen online over multiple channels.

With appropriate rights control, new levels of personalization are possible. For example, broadcasters could break up a standard news program into individual stories, each story having a lead and a full video clip. These stories could then be categorized and filtered through personalized settings to create a unique news broadcast that meets the needs of just one user. For example, all of your news could be filtered to provide only subjects that were of interest to you, could include in-depth coverage, and could be drawn from an international selection of news organizations. No longer would you be forced to get your news from the shallow end of the pond.

Changes Under Way

Having business processes that can scale to handle the number of transactions involved while maintaining performance is critical. Delivery pipelines may soon be able to handle the data volumes required by the new model; but they must be accompanied by a business infrastructure that can support the vast increase in transactions this model entails. The challenge is similar to the transformation of the telephone industry when advancing technology allowed each user to become the operator of his or her own switch to connect a call, instead of depending on legions of operators at switchboards. Call volume, and revenue, increased dramatically. Operators were not scalable for the phone company, but technology was. Advances in the transaction-processing infrastructure followed, until today phone usage and billing are fully automated (even if the bills are difficult to understand—except in comparison to utility bills!).

Media businesses are undergoing dramatic restructuring as they attempt to capitalize on the new opportunities and new services made possible by technology advances. Multibillion-dollar mergers such as AOL–Time Warner and Viacom–CBS illustrate the current movement toward horizontal and vertical integration. The boundaries of broadcasting, computing, and telecommunication have become blurred as the redefining of the media spaces takes place. Major broadcasting and Internet companies are aligning themselves with print and publishing companies to gain access to the supporting assets that enable more personalized service offerings (for the new *any-place any-time when-I-want-it* market). The delivery pipeline now extends across Internet, cable, satellite, terrestrial, telephony, and mobile systems.

The increased opportunity that the new media represent is accompanied by increased risk: the devil is in the details, as they say.

If your infrastructure and business processes can't support the vastly increased volume and complexity of transactions, your company may find itself buried in business, if you get that far. The critical path lies in

- Bridging the gap between the media asset and the customer who wants to access it

- Managing *all* aspects of the media asset—from taking orders, through rights management and contracts, to invoicing—at whatever level of usage the market demands

- Having a system whose performance and scalability can handle the transaction volumes of the new media model

Because customers want to view and interact on the Web, TV, and wireless application protocol (WAP) devices, the media industry requires multiple architectures sharing common repositories. The integration of processes must be managed in a way that enables customers to retrieve what they need, when they want it, in the form that they want, and on any device.

To meet this demand, companies must have total control of their media assets. These must be stored in marketable units in easily searchable databases, with efficient packaging and distribution functionality. Assignment and tracking of rights must be bulletproof, and information must flow easily into back-office systems.

Inverting the one-transaction–many-customers model will vastly increase the number of transactions involved. This increased load can be handled only by an automated system that includes all the business processes involved (order management, asset retrieval and delivery, rights management, usage tracking, invoicing, etc.). Every place where your processes are not automated will require additional personnel and training or additional systems integration.

Pharmaceuticals

The pharmaceutical industry has two distinctive problems. One is the enormous investment required to bring the average drug to market, coupled with the briefness of the period during which that drug is protected by patent. The other is the difficulty of identifying the most effective target(s) for the promotion of drugs.

The Problem of Return on Investment

The past decade has seen astounding growth in the pharmaceutical industry. Advances in science have driven the development of new drugs that can treat such diseases as AIDS and cancer, allowing patients to achieve a quality of life that was unattainable even a few years ago. The aging of the population has created a large market for drugs treating a wide variety of age-related ailments, including high blood pressure, high cholesterol, diabetes, and Alzheimer's disease. In addition, the recent deciphering of the human genome indicates that the rate of scientific progress will continue unabated in the years to come.

However, this progress comes at a price. Costs for pharmaceutical products have been steadily rising—faster than the overall inflation rate—for over a decade; while proponents argue that these products reduce the costs associated with surgery and hospitalization, and also bring significant improvements in the quality of life, others are asking why the costs need to be so high—for example, questioning why an allergy medicine should cost $2 a day when over-the-counter remedies cost more like 30 cents a day, or demanding that AIDS medicines be provided to poorer nations at a fraction of the $10,000 per year price tag that prevails in the United States. To understand these complex pricing issues, we must consider the economics of drug development—illustrated in Fig. 7-2.

Stringent testing, long timescales, and high attrition make drug development risky and expensive. The most frequently quoted estimate is that each drug that is approved costs $500 million, including the costs of compounds that failed during the research process. Obviously the pharmaceutical company needs to recoup that investment and more, and needs to be protected against other companies' exploiting its research to make competitive products. That protection is afforded by the patent process. Under GATT, a company is awarded a 20-year patent from the date of discovery. As Fig. 7-2 shows, on average, more than 10 of those 20 years are gone before the product hits the market. If we assume that sales must equal $2 billion in order to recoup the $500 million development cost and also cover manufacturing costs, sales costs, and reasonable corporate profits, then the drug must exceed $200 million per year in sales. Companies working on "blockbuster" products in important

Pharmaceutical Development and Marketing

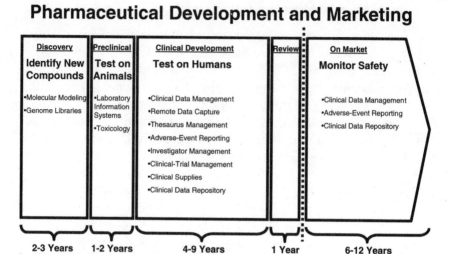

Discovery	Preclinical	Clinical Development	Review	On Market
Identify New Compounds	**Test on Animals**	**Test on Humans**		**Monitor Safety**
•Molecular Modeling •Genome Libraries	•Laboratory Information Systems •Toxicology	•Clinical Data Management •Remote Data Capture •Thesaurus Management •Adverse-Event Reporting •Investigator Management •Clinical-Trial Management •Clinical Supplies •Clinical Data Repository		•Clinical Data Management •Adverse-Event Reporting •Clinical Data Repository
2-3 Years Candidates: 10,000s	**1-2 Years** Targets: 100s	**4-9 Years** 4 Investigational New Drug (IND) Filings	**1 Year**	**6-12 Years** 1 Approved Drug

- **Cost per drug approval: $350 million to $500 million**
- **20-year patent life from discovery to substitution of generic drug**
- **To break even, must make $200 million per year in sales**

Figure 7-2. Pharmaceutical Development and Marketing

therapeutic areas will often target peak annual sales of $1 billion or more. In 2000, the top-selling drug in the world (AstraZeneca's Prilosec for acid-related gastrointestinal disorders) reached more than $6 billion in sales.

The sales targets are reached by "value pricing" the product and marketing it heavily in the most affluent countries. The United States, with 5 percent of the world's population, consumes 40 percent of the world's pharmaceutical products. Japan and western Europe consume another 50 percent, leaving the rest of the world with the remaining 10 percent (largely generic products after patent expiration). Poor countries claim that pharmaceutical companies are garnering excessive profits out of human suffering, while the companies claim that their profits are used to fund past and future R&D. Generally the truth lies somewhere in between.

Reducing Time to Market Brings Enormous Benefits

Whatever the political arguments, the costs of drug development clearly play a huge role in determining the pricing of the eventual product; reducing either the costs or the time involved can bring enormous benefits to all parties. Looked at another way, if a pill can be made for 50 cents and sold for $10 (a representative scenario), then there is precious little benefit in trying to reduce the manufacturing cost to 40 cents. Far more benefit may be realized by increasing the number of consumers for the $10 pill or by lengthening the period during which it may be sold for $10. (The price is typically reduced by 80 percent in the first year after a generic substitute hits the market.) To this end, pharmaceutical companies are trying hard to reduce the time between discovery and approval. Cutting development time by one year will, on average, put $200 million in the bank.

Clinical Trials: The Most Costly and Complex Part of Drug Development

There have been a number of advances in automation of the drug discovery process. Databases containing genetic structures and protein interactions are becoming available, allowing scientists to search through massive amounts of information when looking for drug candidates. These candidate drugs can then be tested using high-throughput screening machines, which yield results an order of magnitude faster than would be possible using manual techniques in the lab. However, the greatest potential benefits for improvement come during the clinical trials process, since this is the most complex, time-consuming, and safety-critical part of drug development. Most companies are therefore focusing the majority of their software investment on systems to improve the collection and management of data during clinical trials.

The Challenges of Collecting Clinical Data

Clinical trials consist of structured experiments to measure the safety and efficacy of the drug in human subjects. Generally the process comprises three phases, as follows:

Phase	Description	Average duration
I	Short safety tests using a small number of subjects	1 year
II	"Dose ranging" studies to find the optimal dosage	2 years
III	Large-scale studies on a wide patient population	3 years

Some of the elapsed time reflects the effort necessary to enroll patients and to measure the effects of the drug in those patients.

However, much time is also spent in preparing for the trials and in processing and analyzing the data they produce. It is in this area that there is the greatest potential for benefit from information technology, for many of today's processes are paper-based, slow, and labor-intensive. To understand why a seemingly simple data processing operation is so complex, consider an example case report form (Fig. 7-3) for a hypothetical clinical trial.

Here several basic data-integrity checks have been violated; but regulations require that the data be entered exactly as they are seen. Any attempt to modify or reject incoming data would be interpreted as suppression of scientific evidence, which in turn could lead the regulatory agencies to reject the submission for drug approval. The computer system must therefore accept the data as shown, then flag anything that violates the integrity rules. Teams of data management professionals then study the flagged data and send appropriate queries back to the investigator responsible for the patient. In the example in Fig. 7-3, they would probably query the missing check

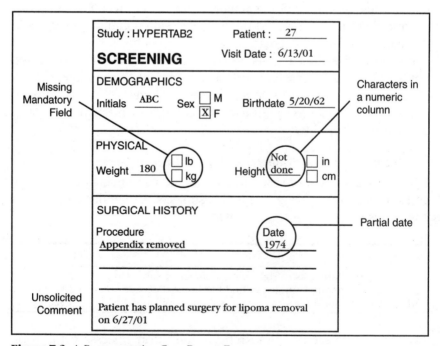

Figure 7-3. A Representative Case Report Form

mark for weight and ask that height be recorded during a future visit. Each such query, on average, costs $90 in administrative time and takes six weeks to resolve.

Electronic Collection of Clinical Data

It is clear that a PC-based system that could validate the data immediately would bring dramatic reductions in both cost and time, and it doesn't seem that it would be difficult to create such a system. However, everything in the pharmaceutical industry is harder than it looks. In addition to the front-end system, a back-end clinical data management system is needed to collect all the data and perform further processing, such as looking up "Appendix removed" in a medical dictionary and turning it into the standard term "Appendectomy." Every data transmission from the front end to the back end needs to be audited, and any differences in data values between the two systems need to be identified and resolved. If a new field needs to be added to the form, that change needs to be broadcast to maybe thousands of PCs. These operational challenges mean that attempts to collect clinical data using stand-alone PCs have failed to show any significant benefits in cost, quality, or time, even after 10 years of trying. Fortunately, there is a new approach that looks much more promising. In pharmaceutical research, as in other industries, the Internet changes everything.

Using the Internet, pharmaceutical companies can now provide data-entry and query-management tools that run dynamically against the same back-end system that is performing all the complex checks, handling the medical dictionaries, and loading data (including lab data) that are collected electronically. This architecture, made possible by huge centralized databases coupled to friendly front-end interfaces on the Web, eliminates intermediate copies of the study definition and of the patient data and thus realizes the benefits of immediate data collection and validation without the historical overhead. Although there are still a number of challenging issues to address, including security, telecommunications infrastructure, and the ever-present regulations on managing electronic signatures for the electronic data, it looks as if the industry is finally set to quit using paper as the primary medium for data collection. Software vendors can now provide secure end-to-end solutions reaching from the physician's office at the front end to a clinical trials system at the back end, enabling clinical data to be collected securely and efficiently. These efficiency savings will allow patients to benefit from new drugs more quickly; they will also allow a quicker return on R&D investment by the pharmaceutical company, thereby leading to lower costs.

The Problem of Promotion

The costs of prescription drugs have been rising rapidly in the United States. This is especially true of drugs prescribed mostly for the elderly: Prices for such drugs rose 25.2 percent from January 1994 to January 1999, while the overall inflation rate for that period was 12.8 percent. Pharmacy costs rose from 7 percent of health maintenance organization (HMO) medical costs to 12.5 percent between 1990 and 1997. Meanwhile, the profits of drug companies were running well ahead of the average for the *Fortune* 500. A consequence of these trends has been high political sensitivity to the issue of drug prices, which figured prominently during 2000 in both the Gore and the Bush presidential campaigns.

This is a matter of extreme delicacy for pharmaceutical manufacturers, which naturally want to maximize their profits but are loath to alienate the public or the politicians that represent it. One aspect of the matter is that drug companies risk simply losing the business of consumers who can no longer afford their products.

The truly distinctive problem for the pharmaceutical industry is that the consumers of drugs have little influence in choosing the drugs they are to consume. Traditionally, physicians have made these choices; presumably they have typically prescribed the drugs that they expected to be most effective in relation to the patients' conditions, but sometimes, no doubt—for patients in financial difficulty—they have prescribed drugs that were less effective but also less expensive.

From a 21st-century standpoint, the traditional arrangement looks not only simple but terribly innocent. In order to understand the full complexity of the current situation, we need to examine the role of each of the many parties involved. To treat them in a logical order, we'll follow the path of a pill on its way from the manufacturer to your stomach.

To promote their products, *pharmaceutical manufacturers* have traditionally sent out sales reps, usually armed with free samples, to make personal calls on physicians. According to *The Economist*,[8] pharmaceutical manufacturers employ 63,000 sales reps—at a cost that amounts to one-half of the $15.5 billion the companies spend per year on marketing. But companies are increasingly impatient with this way of promoting their products, suspecting that the results do not justify the cost.

Manufacturers have turned increasingly to advertising, whether to physicians or directly to the public. Direct-to-consumer (DTC) advertising used to be confined to over-the-counter drugs; in recent years, it has extended to what we call prescription drugs, and ads for these drugs have increasingly appeared in magazines, on radio and television, and via direct mailings. Drug manufacturers' annual budgets for marketing to consumers have risen in total from about $12 million in 1989 to about $2.5 billion today; as these numbers suggest, companies find DTC marketing highly cost-effective. Manufacturers have also experimented with acquiring pharmaceutical benefit management (PBM) companies (which we discuss later), but only one such integration—Merck-Medco—survives.

Physicians, within or outside hospitals, have traditionally welcomed the free samples provided by the manufacturers' sales reps, although the benefits may usually have passed directly to their patients. But their prescribing practices were probably influenced more by what they knew about candidate drugs than by which pills happened to lurk in their desk drawers. Regardless, recent research indicates that many physicians are strongly influenced by other physicians whose opinions they respect. This suggests that a major concern for pharmaceutical companies is to identify, and to concentrate their marketing efforts on, these "referee" physicians.

Even for these physicians, however, their autonomy in prescribing is not what it once was. Recent decades have seen several developments that impinge on that autonomy from various directions. One such development is the growing influence of *insurance providers* (including *HMOs* and *health plans*), which are concerned that patients be treated with drugs that are not necessarily the most effective but that are the most *cost*-effective. This is also a reasonable attitude for patients, especially those who are uninsured

---

[8]"Rebirth of a salesman," *The Economist*, April 14, 2001, p. 62.

or are covered by a plan that requires copayments that vary from one medication to another. However, all parties to such arrangements need to weigh the costs of medication against the costs of the potential medical consequences if drugs are not prescribed—and taken as prescribed. But this concern is tempered for insurance providers by the recognition that the patient's coverage—and its costs—may pass to another provider before any such consequence materializes.

Enterprises in this category generally develop *formularies*, which are lists of recommended drugs; as a rule, insurance coverage for a prescription depends on the drug's inclusion in the insurer's formulary. Other sources of formularies are *pharmaceutical benefit management (PBM) companies*, whose initial purpose for existence was to design and evaluate programs for patient-care management; this logically meant monitoring the cost-effectiveness of medicines and the prescribing habits of physicians and reporting those findings to interested parties. Some PBMs are independent; others have belonged to HMOs; one—Merck-Medco—belongs to a drug manufacturer.

(Many of these enterprises are promoting physician use of personal digital assistants (PDAs) to provide them with instant access to current formulary terms, meaning that physicians and patients will increasingly have access to pricing and reimbursement information at the time the prescription is written. Drug companies themselves are rapidly expanding their use of e-mail to convey drug information to doctors.)

The typical insurance outfit will contract with a pharmacy chain, which will guarantee drug discounts in return for the (more or less) exclusive business of the consumers insured under the plan(s) in question. However, such arrangements are illegal in some states. Some insurance plans have also begun to hold doctors partly responsible for the costs of their prescriptions, exacting penalties when those costs exceed specified limits but issuing rebates when costs are held down; although this moves the doctors in the direction of cost-effectiveness, the AMA considers it unethical because it encourages doctors to profit by slanting their prescribing decisions. When a physician prescribes a drug that has a comparably effective but less expensive alternative, the pharmacist might in theory substitute the alternative without explicit authorization from the physician, but the AMA opposes this practice too.

With regard to prescription drugs, *consumers* usually cannot make the decision to buy, but they can lobby their physicians; surveys show that nearly all physicians have received queries from patients about drugs they have seen advertised—and that almost all such queries specified a brand name. Increasingly, also, consumers are turning to the Internet to purchase drugs internationally when such drugs may not be purchased in the United States except as prescribed; however, this practice is illegal.

In short, the influences over a drug-consumption decision usually involve a snake's nest of interwoven and sometimes conflicting motives. To cope with this tangle, pharmaceutical manufacturers—in particular—need sophisticated database software to maintain and manipulate their rapidly increasing data volumes, and sophisticated data-mining software to analyze the data and identify the most rewarding targets for their marketing efforts.

Data regarding prescriptions are available from companies including Information Resources, Inc., and IMS Health. Analytical needs can be met by off-the-shelf data-mining software. The results of such analysis will feed logically into any e-business suite, the marketing and sales functions of which will be essential for manufacturers that hope to profit by exploiting the intelligence they have wrung from their data stores.

Telecommunications
Changing to a Customer-Centric View

Communications service providers, once monopolies with a focus on building networks, are changing the way they do business. Stiff competition, new products and services, and a convergence of technologies have resulted in an about-face in the communications industry—from a network-centric model to a customer-centric model.

The recent history of the communications market has been determined by deregulation and technological advances. Traditionally, telecommunications applications were defined according to the connection to the network. Network applications were central to operations, and other systems were considered informational or, like the customer, peripheral. Typically systems were divided between business support systems (BSS), like marketing and order taking, and operations support systems (OSS), like order processing and provisioning. OSS applications were designed to meet static business needs. The present generation of OSS originates in the management of fixed-line telephony networks, which are experiencing reduced profitability. The areas of growth and investment are wireless networks, mobile internets, digital subscriber line (DSL) services, Internet application services, and high-capacity optical backbone networks. The current generation of OSS and BSS cannot keep pace with the rate of change demanded by this dynamic marketplace.

The market now demands that telecom companies know their customers and focus on customer care, rapid customer acquisition, customer retention, and cost reduction. This means, for example, providing solutions like workforce scheduling. Rather than itself setting the time and day of a dispatch ("Please be at home from 9:00 A.M. to noon on July 3 so we can turn on your service"), a world-class service provider must let the customer set the time and day of the appointment, then schedule its resources to accommodate the customer. Customer relationship management meets communications.

Industry Challenges

While the industry recognizes the need for these changes, they induce culture shock in many companies, where direction is still set by the IT department. IT does not have the breadth of vision required to create new business processes. Understaffed and barely able to manage the integration of point solutions across a plethora of legacy systems, IT is even less well equipped to drive the use of new strategies across other departments. The Peter Principle has met e-Darwinism in the telecommunications industry, fortunately driving these decisions up to the C-level executive where they belong.

Motivated by the desire for CRM solutions, specifically for managing business-to-business (B2B) and business-to-consumer (B2C) relationships, telecom companies have realized that, in order to serve their customers, they must know who those customers are and what they want. But they have attacked the customer space with point solutions. They have not implemented a global CRM solution; they haven't known how to do it.

The communications industry was one of the first to computerize, but now its many legacy systems and the associated business processes make adopting new technology difficult. In many ways new companies face fewer hurdles than mature companies on the road to becoming e-businesses.

The complexity of the industry and the rapid change it is undergoing present a myriad of issues that must be resolved with new business practices and new software tools. A quick list of them includes

- Lack of integration of OSS and BSS applications. Each product or service can have a separate and independent method for taking and processing orders. This complexity is exacerbated by rapid growth in the number and types of products and services available. Traditional "systems integration" can quickly become a company-crushing burden.

- Product and subscriber data that are buried in OSS applications. Information that could constructively be shared is in fact inseparable from the application that captured it. Such data must be extracted from the various OSS and BSS applications, scrubbed to remove redundancy, and moved into a shared CRM database.

- Multiplicity of legacy systems. Migration and implementation issues are a critical challenge for telecom companies as they try to change their business focus.

- Special inventory needs. Automation has been retarded by inventory applications that do not provide for network information like circuits and IP addresses. Correcting this deficiency would enable the company to know, for example, which customers were affected by a failed circuit, promoting more proactive customer service.

CRM for the Communications Industry

New technologies, Internet-enabled applications, and the deregulation of providers have created a competitive environment in which service boundaries have blurred, more opportunities are being created in wireless and data than in traditional telecommunication services, and the market is consolidating into fewer, larger, more international companies. There are clear opportunities for CRM support of next-generation services such as broadband (including cable modems, DSL, frame relay, and wireless), mobile entertainment, and prepaid wireless, for both the consumer and wholesale markets.

The communications industry requires a CRM solution that reengineers and integrates legacy communications processes, surmounting the barriers created by their history. CRM applications that support communications require functionality that embodies high-level end-to-end business flows for sales and revenue operations; monitoring, repairing, and maintaining networks; and creating network-to-network segments (electronically continuous portions of networks).

CRM Application Goals

To meet the market's needs, to enable cost savings, and to increase revenue, CRM applications for the communications industry must

- Enable rapid service delivery
- Provide a comprehensive and unified view of the customer
- Reduce ownership costs
- Integrate and automate order management and provisioning
- Support new products and services

Enable Rapid Service Delivery. A communications-enabling CRM solution must reduce the time to market from months to weeks. A critical need is to be able to bundle services on a single order, with information flow-through to provisioning, yet be able to dynamically reconfigure the order later if necessary. Communications companies in North America modify 67 percent of all orders taken within seven days of order placement.

Provide a Comprehensive and Unified View of the Customer. Traditionally, communication companies supported a product-centric model, with billing and ordering systems that varied with the product or service. Today, communication companies need to offer bundled services to each customer and bill only once. The solution is a unified view of the customer across all lines of service.

CRM software must help telecommunications companies understand and become proactive in dealing with their customers. For example, integrated service-management functionality could enable a company to monitor the performance of the services it offers and take action if the performance falls below certain levels. The system could track every network resource, service component, and customer. Real-time alarm and performance data could be correlated with a customer's services to enable proactive responses to situations. Such a knowledge base would benefit both the company and its customers. For example, the company would gain data for analysis of real-time use and capacity. Customers could view their networks and understand how their services were performing, and could use self-service to order additional bandwidth if necessary.

Reduce Ownership Costs. Legacy OSS applications have typically been developed over several decades. They were designed to meet the slowly changing needs of the fixed-line telephony customer; cost of ownership was probably not a big consideration. As the communications industry matured, point solutions were added for OSS/BSS needs such as provisioning, fault and performance management, and billing. While these solutions improved functionality, they introduced greater integration challenges, and the result was increased long-term cost of ownership. Companies no longer want or can afford solutions that demand integration consultancies. They want applications that can be configured to meet evolving needs, not customized to meet their needs at one point in time.

Integrate and Automate Order Management and Provisioning. Today's market demands speed and efficiency that only integration can provide—the billing system must be able to handle such diversity as charges based on content, volume, duration, or time and payment options that include prepayment, real-time payment, and postpayment. Order management must be able to reduce a complex order to smaller tasks that can be provisioned, fulfill both the subscription service and any shippable items (e.g., cell phones) from inventory, and activate the service.

Support New Products and Services. Communications service providers are executing strategies to become more than circuit or communications pipeline providers. They are meeting network demand, pushing content and applications to their customers, and taking on the broader role of providers of voice, data, video, entertainment, appliance, and network applications—anytime and anywhere. VDSL is being rolled out not to give customers faster

Internet browsing capabilities but to serve as a distribution medium for video and entertainment content. CATV companies are integrating voice services into their entertainment and Internet services and are already considered video entertainment distributors. CRM applications must be broad enough and flexible enough to support changing business models.

Summary

Simplification and integration are key here. Every telecommunications company must do business as a single company, not as a conglomerate of disparate products and services. Telecommunications companies face many challenges to integrating and automating e-business processes, but those who do it first stand to gain considerably over those who don't. Changing to a customer-centric model will provide these companies with a broadband rush of insight into themselves and their customers, fueled with new Web-enabled CRM tools such as business intelligence tied to sales, marketing, and service applications, and flow-through order management and provisioning. Companies that cannot or choose not to implement their own CRM solutions will find relief in the form of hosted services. Having been down the systems integration road farther than most, telecommunications companies can be expected to be enthusiastic adopters of out-of-the-box solutions with extensive configuration options, yet these solutions must still address industry-specific needs and target markets within the communications industry. The industry is poised to reap the productivity gains that its advances have enabled.

8

Changing the Business—Getting from Here to There

Accelerated response, reduced complexity, lowered expenses, heightened productivity, global enablement, self-service, management by fact. Broadened participation by the trading community, industry-focused solutions, software as a service. A platform for growth, an engine for cutting costs—for up economies, for down economies, for all economies.

It sounds great. But how does Company XYZ get from where it is—now—to the goal: successful implementation of a global single instance enabling rapid response? What steps must it take?

Try these nine:

1. Create a crisis.

2. Senior managers, lead!

3. Forget current complexities; implement the future.

4. Prepare to sustain casualties.

5. Pluck the low-hanging fruit.

6. Share vision, share ownership.

7. Use standard products and technologies.

8. Create a platform.

9. Return to step 1. Remember, the journey is the destination.

Step 1: Create a Crisis

When Cortés landed at Tabasco in 1519, he and his men confronted disease, homesickness, low morale, and Aztec forces that outnumbered the Spaniards by perhaps 5,000 to 1. So—naturally— Cortés burnt his ships, leaving his men with a simple choice: dare or die.

By now, most major companies have taken a few meaningful steps toward the new world of the Internet. As for the rest, their executives are now in the shoes—well, the sabotons—of Cortés. They must burn their boats and set out on a path to the future. Some of their competitors are already moving in that direction.

Burning the boats is not burning the plan; to the contrary, it's a statement of one essential element of the plan. A superb opportunist, Cortés wanted to keep all his options open . . . as long as they were options for success. For him, burning the boats meant setting a direction and curtailing time-wasting debate. The point of the crisis he created was to focus and motivate his troops, not to convince them that he was off his head.

The e-transformation can profit from *lots* of planning. At the beginning, however, it's not essential to know exactly what the enterprise will look like two years from now, or exactly how it's going to get from here to there. What the executive *does* need is to understand the business and its potential and to have some idea of what it will be once it's enabled for the Internet.

Step 2: Senior Managers, Lead!

Tactical technology issues can be pushed down or staffed out for decisions. Most companies undergoing this transition will form implementation teams, working groups, and program management offices, and will try to involve evaluation committees, the e-business suite vendor, implementation and business management consultants, and the end users of the system. But moving the business onto the Internet, and beyond that onto an e-business suite, requires strategic decision of the highest order. Concomitant decisions must be taken rapidly, at the most senior levels, and escalations from lower levels are to be encouraged.

Decisions taken during this journey can lead to expenses that will range, in some cases, into the billions of dollars; to business processes that are changed beyond recognition; to the consolidation of multiple lines of business. Senior management *must lead* or be exposed as incompetent. This journey, from the Tower of Babel to an integrated and rationalized system for business automation, is the most important opportunity top executives will ever have to understand their businesses, to take control of them, and to ensure that they will scale without meaningful limits.

Step 3: Implement the Future

Too often, business transformations are retarded by the need, real or imagined, to understand all the current systems, processes, and data—to assess the impacts of the conversion and the training needs it poses. It can be easy to spend too much time trying to comprehend past or present business processes predicated on local systems and incomplete automation. To the extent that this slows down the company's transition to the future, it risks condemning that transition to failure, even though it may be completed . . . too late.

Moreover, working toward a full understanding of the systems to be replaced can prejudice decision makers in favor of simply reproducing their functionality on the Internet platform. Although this will rarely be the optimal path forward for the company, it will exercise a seductive charm on executives and teams that have been exhorted, to the point of exhaustion, to "destroy your business." After all, it is the path of least conceptual resistance, and it provides a welcome illusion of transformation.

Executives who are planning to phase in an e-business suite will necessarily concern themselves with how components of that suite will interact with applications that are already in use, and/or with which current applications can most constructively continue to serve as the environment gradually changes. By contrast, executives should minimize any concern with existing business processes and concentrate instead on processes that will serve the company's future needs.

Try to understand past and present systems to the extent that is strictly necessary. But implement the future.

Step 4: Prepare to Sustain Casualties

For now, there is no change on the business horizon that compares in importance to the e-business revolution. Businesses must begin it, and having begun it must see it through to a logical conclusion. Obstacles must be shattered. And this reminds me of days spent crabbing, in my youth, on the Connecticut shore.

The fashion, when you go crabbing, is to throw your crabs into a bucket in the middle of the fishing boat; but—oddly—nobody bothers to put a lid on the bucket, even though the crabs develop a foul temper and will claw, pinch, and bite. Why no lid? Because the crabs are conformists: if one crab is inspired to climb the side of the bucket, the other crabs grab at it and pull it back down into the crowd at the bottom. What's the result? Nobody breaks out.

People are like crabs, more or less. Everybody knows ways to do lots of things and will often turn, by preference, to a way that works pretty reliably. But the point of the Internet is to break the mold. So the migration is full of challenges:

- To keep the conformist crabs from dragging the soldier-of-fortune crabs back down

- To channel the conservative impulses of the conformists in such ways that the soldiers of fortune tend to struggle constructively toward the goal of e-transformation, not away from it

- To channel the innovative impulses of the adventurous crabs in such ways that the conformists are inspired to follow them when they see them headed in a promising direction

What are the possible obstacles to the e-business transformation?

- People
- Systems
- Data
- Interfaces

People

See my previous remarks on crabs.

Systems

If the current systems are hideously complex, don't labor to understand them. Switch them off. In any case where the functionality provided is indispensable, write throwaway code to serve as a bridge to the future system; then, as possible, develop a simple and rational way to replace that functionality using the Internet. Once the new way is ready, *then* switch off the old one.

Data

The essence of data deployment for the Internet Age is a single global database with a single record for every logical member of the business's trading community—and for every other business entity, if possible. Existing data that can migrate into such a structure should be encouraged to do so; existing data that cannot should be thrown overboard, as a rule, though information that is clearly crucial can be entered manually into the new system.

Remember, the transformation needs to reach a logical conclusion, and without delay. Executives would be surprised at how much accumulated data can be thrown away. Staff who think they need certain data will fight to retain those data, but they are almost always mistaken.

Interfaces

The word *interface* usually means *yet another bespoke system.* Some third-party applications (e.g., for credit scoring) will not be obsoleted by the e-transformation, because their specificity and complexity argue against incorporating them into a general business suite. But most such products, and the interfaces to and among them, will effectively be replaced by e-business suites. With the others, it makes sense to weigh their importance against the danger they pose of delaying the e-business transformation.

Step 5: Pluck the Low-Hanging Fruit

Well . . . if you're lying on your back looking up through the branches, these fruit won't look so low. But they are the prizes to be gathered first by every business that aspires to global enablement for the Internet, because of their intrinsic importance and because the implementation of any one of these is a milestone along a sensible path to e-business:

- Global sales forecast
- Global lead position
- Global order position
- Global inventory position
- Global marketing expenditure
- Global contracts
- Collaborative sales automation for suppliers, partners, customers, and employees

The processes that enable these items constitute a natural first step on the road to rapid response. They are already familiar to most businesses, though perhaps not on the scale indicated here. Handled intelligently, they will produce demonstrable signs of business transformation, and they promise relatively high impact for relatively low effort.

Step 6: Share Vision, Share Ownership

Take care that involvement in the transformation is spread as broadly as possible among the people whose lives will be affected by it. Consider the merits of a system that distributes ownership among four levels:

- Those accountable
- Those responsible
- Those consulted
- Those informed

Those Accountable For any major task, only one person can be accountable. The decision as to who gets responsibility at this level needs to rest on an understanding of the job to be done and of the candidates to do it; in some cases a Patton will succeed more conspicuously, in others an Eisenhower. Often the most likely to succeed is the hardest-working, most obsessive, roll-up-your-sleeves, take-no-prisoners person that the organization can offer.

Those Responsible For every major success or failure, there will be many people responsible. For the e-transformation, the key stakeholders are the top executives, the technical team, systems consultants, and so forth. It is important that the vision, as well as the responsibility, be shared among these folks—and that they sign up for a set not of goals but of commitments.

Those Consulted These include technical experts, business-process consultants, prospective end users, and others whose views and expertise are needed but who cannot reasonably be brought aboard as full-time contributors.

Those Informed These are typically parties, often managers, whose responsibilities and concerns hinge in some way on the progress of the project, but who have no part in the decision-making process.

Business will need something like this four-level stratification in order to move forward briskly and secure the operational efficiencies that will enable rapid response and the competitive advantages they confer.

Step 7: Use Standard Products and Technologies

The argument for standardization is overwhelming. The technology that enables the Internet, and many of the technologies that exploit it, are already world standards. No company has much to gain by marching to its own drummer when the partners and customers it hopes to do business with are marching together to a different rhythm.

This argues for using products that are attuned to recognized technology standards. Beyond that, it argues for using products that have not been modified to meet the supposed needs of a single purchaser. In the service of corporate efficiency, the Web is enabling the progressive interpenetration of every business's processes by those of its channel partners, its suppliers, and its corporate customers; but the elegant interweaving we can foresee will be sadly disfigured if business processes that need to interfuse prove actually to conflict.

The Internet has served this ball into the court of the software vendors, and return of service is under way. Software vendors have the potential and the responsibility to become the arbiters of business-process standards for the third millennium, and if they need industry expertise they must draw on it as appropriate. Let them do what they are in business to do—develop the software. And let their customers focus on their own core competencies, not spend their time and treasure reworking the software they have purchased. Let the business world learn to speak a common language.

The benefits of such an approach extend well beyond more effective coordination within and between businesses. They include

- Reduced implementation times and expense
- Easier upgrades
- Ready access to pools of labor with needed skills and experience
- Reduced workloads for customer IT groups
- Greater participation in corporate processes, because they will be more accessible to trading community members that are using the same technology standards
- Greater scalability
- Improved performance on remote networks

Step 8: Create a Platform

The e-transformation is not a sprint; it's a marathon. For this reason, the task force needs an early win to sustain morale, build confidence, and validate ROI projections. This is part of the justification for steps 5 and 7.

However, any reassuring early result needs to be realized on a sound platform that will accommodate ready extension to the next business flow, the next functional module, the next line of business. Because the process is going to prove to be iterative.

Step 9: Return to Step 1

Pass GO. Collect $200.

Successive trips around this cycle will progressively confirm the company's metamorphosis into a full-fledged e-business, even as the definition of *e-business* is itself evolving. Even so, the first pass through steps 1 through 8 is the most important, given that it comprises the deployment of the first Web-enabled business flow and a commitment to a specific information architecture. The company cannot afford to jeopardize this architecture and its accompanying platform; it pays to reduce the scope of the next iteration if it poses a serious risk to the emerging e-business foundation.

Can we foresee how the most fully enabled Web businesses will operate a decade from now? Only, to quote Mark Twain, "as through a glass eye, darkly." The road to rapid response is a long one. Any company that undertakes this transformation *now*, with conviction and intelligence, has the potential to pace the world in 2010.

Appendix

E-Leaders—Case Studies

This section discusses eight enterprises that are in various stages of the transition from traditional business to e-business. Their stories are different; their histories vary in length and complexity. Indeed, BellSouth connects directly to the industrial revolution and the dawn of the information age. Hewlett-Packard dates from the birth of Silicon Valley, and Xerox created the copier business. JDS Uniphase, on the other hand, is but a few years old, born of the technology age.

What ties these companies together—the theme their stories share— is the way they have confronted the demands of the times and the opportunities of the Internet and decided to become e-businesses. Each is simplifying and redefining its business processes to achieve global integration within and across functional groups. Global Web access to applications and information, comprehensive views of the processes by which they live or die, a 360° view of customer activity, greater efficiency, greater focus on the customer, reduced costs and increased revenues—these are the goals, and these companies are well on their way. They intend to manage themselves better and manage their information better, and to do it with less effort. And they are ready for new growth because they are implementing solutions that are scalable.

These companies and companies like them are showing the way.

BellSouth

Industry	Telecommunications
Founded	1984
Employees	103,900*
FY 2000 revenue	$26.1 billion
Market capitalization	$72.1 billion[†]

*Includes figures for Cingular Wireless.
[†]All tabulated market-capitalization figures in this appendix are for late January 2002.

BellSouth provides voice and data services in the United States and other countries. Its principal offerings include network access, information access, and local exchange and intra-LATA (local access and transport area) long distance services. In the residential market, BellSouth offers digital subscriber line (DSL) high-speed Internet access, advanced voice features, and other services. For business customers, the company provides broadband data and e-commerce solutions. E-business centers in Georgia and Florida provide Web-hosting solutions that include storage on demand, managed security, content distribution, caching, disaster recovery, and full support for applications service providers—all in hardened facilities that can withstand disasters, as they did with the category 4 hurricane Andrew. In south Florida, BellSouth has built the most advanced Internet exchange in the country. The BellSouth Florida multimedia Internet exchange (MIX) is where Internet service providers, Web hosting firms, and other large Internet-related businesses hand off data to one another.

BellSouth owns 40 percent of Cingular Wireless, the nation's second largest wireless company, which provides wireless voice and data services. Cingular's data service covers more than 93 percent of the urban business population. The service gives paging users the ability to initiate and respond to messages to or from other pagers, fax machines, and telephones via Internet e-mail.

In 2001 the company expanded its DSL services by teaming with Dell Computer to offer DSL-equipped PCs.

History

By 1982 the AT&T Bell system had grown to $155 billion in assets, with over one million employees.[1] On August 24, 1982, after seven years of negotiation, the Bell system was split apart. AT&T kept its long distance service, Western Electric, Bell Labs, the newly formed AT&T Technologies, and AT&T Consumer Products; it divested itself of the regional Bell operating companies, effective January 1, 1984. The operating companies were consolidated into seven large entities. South Central Bell and Southern Bell became BellSouth, which began life with 96,000 employees and $21.5 billion in assets. The two

---

[1] By comparison, Microsoft in mid-2001 had cash and short-term investments totaling about $32 billion.

companies maintained separate operations until 1991, when they were combined into BellSouth Telecommunications.

BellSouth aggressively expanded and upgraded its analog networks to broadband digital networks and offered new services. In 1984 it activated the first cellular systems in the southeastern United States, and in 1985 it launched five new high-speed, high-capacity data services. Business agreements on four continents soon helped BellSouth expand its networks and services into France, Italy, Guatemala, and India. By this time the company also owned a majority interest in Australia's largest independent paging and answering-service company.

In 1990 BellSouth retired its last electromechanical switch, becoming the first Bell company to complete the transition to an all-electronic network. It also became the world's first cellular company to hit the 500,000-customer mark. The 1990s saw cellular service expand into Venezuela and Chile, and BellSouth became part of a consortium that was awarded a license to become the second Australian telecommunications company, providing wireline, wireless, and satellite service. In 1995 BellSouth was adding a new customer somewhere in the world every 15 seconds.

In 1999 the company offered the first integrated package that included Internet, wireless, paging, and local phone service with calling features—all on one bill and with one number for service. The company also completed an alliance with Qwest Communications International that, within six months, generated 27 contracts worth $250 million in business for broadband services. (BellSouth bought a 10 percent position in Qwest for $3.5 billion; Qwest began buying back BellSouth's stake in 2001.)

By 2000 BellSouth was adding a new customer somewhere in the world every 10 seconds.

BellSouth now serves more than 45 million total customers in the nine southern states, Latin America, South America, and Europe. By the end of 2001 it will have nearly 600,000 asynchronous DSL (ADSL) customers.

The *e* in Corporate and the *e* in Customer

BellSouth formed a shared services center nearly three years ago to streamline its operations. The use of Oracle financial management software has enabled BellSouth to make significant improvements in all the key areas of financial efficiency, from accounts payable processing to an Internet-based employee expense management system.

Oracle supply-chain software is being used to completely transform the way BellSouth plans, manages, and procures all items necessary for the day-to-day running of its business. BellSouth is also implementing an ordering system that is integrated across all business units. This system uses Oracle CRM software to provide a single view of all BellSouth services and products that any customer owns.

This facilitates other capabilities such as comprehensive and scalable self-service, which has been part of BellSouth's initiative to provide customers with Internet-based interactive applications that allow them to do much more of their business with BellSouth via the Web. This strategy was based on direct feedback from customers. In a survey of customers who use the Internet, 79 percent said they wanted product pricing and availability information on the BellSouth Web site; 75 percent said they wanted the ability to review their monthly bills; 72 percent said they wanted to order products over the Web, and 50 percent said they wanted "solution-adviser" products.

The interactive customer service applications, located at www.bellsouth.com, are useful to residential and business customers and prospects. Customers will find a complete catalog of products and services on BellSouth's Web site. In addition to detailed product descriptions, the catalog includes instructions for use and location-specific product and pricing information. Customers may review current and previous bills and access links to notes on payment alternatives, explanations of charges, and answers to common billing questions.

For small-business customers, the Solution Advisor provides instant recommendations for customized telecommunications solutions. Using customer responses to an interactive questionnaire about specific business requirements, BellSouth's online small-business specialist recommends specific products, with pricing tailored for the specific locale.

"This is an excellent example of a telco creatively reinventing itself around its customers' requirements," said Traver Kennedy, worldwide director of telecommunications research at Aberdeen Group, a Boston-based industry analysis firm. "By providing this feature-rich Internet solution, BellSouth is delivering improved customer service directly into the hands of its customers—choice, convenience and control—as it delivers on its corporate strategy and leadership vision."

EMC

Industry	Data storage systems
Founded	1979
Employees	23,000
FY 2000 revenue	$8.87 billion
Market capitalization	$37.5 billion

The University of California, Berkeley, recently reported that the amount of new information being generated is expected to double annually.[2] During the years 2001 and 2002, more new information will have been created than over the entire previous history of the planet—more than 90 percent of it digital. Many companies will find themselves in the position of having amounts of information that are too large to manage yet too valuable to ignore. This is good news for EMC Corporation, the world leader in systems that store, protect, move, manage, and access this explosion of content.

EMC offers hardware storage systems, networked storage products, storage software, and best-practice information for the deployment of its solutions. EMC has also formed alliances with leading software, networking, and service companies, including KPMG, Microsoft, SAP, and Oracle, to better serve its customers. EMC has industry-specific expertise that extends to energy, government, finance, health care, manufacturing, retail, and telecommunications.

EMC has the world's largest storage-dedicated direct sales and service force. The company supports its customers 24 × 7 by combining advanced remote-service technology with the hands-on expertise of skilled service teams. Using the latest diagnostic technology—including telecommunications links that continuously

---

[2]In 2000 EMC sponsored a study by the School of Information Management and Systems at the University of California, Berkeley, to determine how much information exists and how much new information is being created every day. The findings of the study were published at http://www.sims.berkeley.edu/research/projects/how-much-info/.

monitor and report on the status of each installed system—EMC's built-in service approach is designed to detect any error before it renders data unavailable.

The future, according to EMC, is the universal data tone. When you pick up the phone, you expect to hear that familiar tone that tells you that the phone is on and that you can now easily call someone across town or across time zones. The universal dial tone was a concept that transformed the telephone from a mere invention to a globally significant innovation.

EMC believes that in the years ahead, from the palm of your hand, your living room, your workspace, or your favorite vacation spot, you will be able to access the storage infrastructure and get a universal data tone. No matter where you are, or what application you're running, you'll have access to precisely the information you need when you need it. The principles behind the universal data tone will be the same as those behind the universal dial tone—any-to-any communication, reliability, established and efficient global management, interoperability, security, standard access devices, and scalability.

"Hello. Press 1 if you would like to download all the information currently in existence. Press 2 for. . . ."

History

EMC Corporation was founded in 1979 by Richard Egan and Roger Marino. Egan, the first CEO, had worked at Intel; he and Marino began by selling office desks, but they soon took advantage of the Intel connection, moving into selling Intel-compatible memory. One prospect wanted Prime-compatible memory instead; this led to the development of EMC's first product, a memory board introduced in 1981.

In 1986 EMC went public at $16.50 per share. At that time the company was also manufacturing add-on storage for machines from Data General, DEC, HP, IBM, and Wang, and it next began to expand into disk storage. In 1987 it introduced solid-state disk (SSD) storage for minicomputers. SSD devices use controllers and memory disks to emulate conventional disks; they contain no moving parts and are therefore much faster. In 1988, the company hired Mike Ruettgers to address quality and service issues; this was timely, as four months later the company was hit by its biggest crisis when newly shipped EMC devices began to crash all over the country.

Eventually the company determined that the problem lay with disks supplied by NEC. However, it was obvious that EMC's quality-control efforts had also failed. EMC replaced all the defective products at a cost of $100 million, which nearly drove it into bankruptcy, but at the same time demonstrated the company's commitment to customer welfare. The effort marked the birth at EMC of the religion of quality control.

In 1990 EMC revised its strategy to focus on mainframe disk storage systems; in doing so, it canceled nine major product lines that were generating 80 percent of its revenues. For the struggle to come, its weapon was the revolutionary Symmetrix Integrated Cached Disk Array, which used RAID (redundant arrays of inexpensive disks) configurations to outdo IBM in reliability, performance, and price. Within three years, EMC had displaced Big Blue as the leading supplier of storage for IBM's own mainframes.

Ruettgers had proven himself. In 1992 he replaced Egan as CEO. His next epiphany was inspired by a data-center manager's complaints about the difficulties of data communication among computers from multiple manufacturers. Ruettgers recognized that what was needed was "open storage," a single storage system that could hold data from lots of incompatible computers and return it, on inquiry, in the form suited to the querying machine.

EMC introduced the Symmetrix 3000, the first open storage system, in July 1995.[3] Sales hit $200 million in that year, $800 million in 1996, and more than $2 billion in 1998. Meanwhile, the company had introduced SRDF (Symmetrix Remote Data Facility), its first software product, in 1994. Since then, EMC's revenues—and especially its profits—have benefited from the rapid growth of its software business. By 2000, with $1.5 billion in annual software revenues, EMC was the 16th-largest software developer in the world and the world leader in storage-management software.

In 2000 EMC's total consolidated revenues grew 32 percent to $8.87 billion. Information storage revenues (which made up 93 percent of the total) grew at an accelerating pace each quarter: 34 percent in the first

---

[3]EMC systems now interoperate with nearly 400 server models, 40 operating systems, 81 storage software products, and more than 145 networking elements.

quarter, 43 percent in the second, 47 percent in the third, and 50 percent in the fourth, EMC's highest quarterly storage growth rate in nearly six years. Internationally, EMC's information storage revenues grew even faster, reaching 67 percent year-to-year growth in the fourth quarter.

In response to the 1989 crisis, EMC's adjusted share price had fallen as low as 5.7 cents. At its peak on September 25, 2000, of $104.9375, the stock had appreciated from that trough by a factor of 1840; this included the greatest one-calendar-decade rise in the history of the NYSE, by a factor of 806 from 1990 to 2000. By late 2001 the stock had fallen, in accord with the market, as low as $10.01; this is likely to prove its bear-market low.

In 2000, according to a report from International Data Corporation (IDC), EMC Corporation was first in the rapidly growing worldwide disk storage systems market, gaining more market share than any other supplier and extending its lead in several major information storage segments. According to Gartner Dataquest, EMC now commands 33 percent of the $17.8 billion market for external storage systems; Compaq has 10.4 percent, and IBM has 7.8 percent. Other competitors are Hewlett-Packard, Hitachi, and Sun. Gartner Dataquest projects that the market for external storage systems will grow to $51 billion by 2005. In the market for storage software, EMC has extended its lead in 2000 by nearly six points, to 25.5 percent, according to Gartner Dataquest.

EMC is represented by more than 100 sales offices and distribution partners in more than 50 countries.

EMC's Roadmap

EMC chose a two-pronged approach to reworking and modernizing its business systems. The first phase focused primarily on ERP functionality. In the second phase, EMC is establishing a worldwide standard for CRM based upon Oracle's E-Business Suite.

In 1999 EMC selected Oracle as the software provider for its financial, distribution, and manufacturing application software. The objective of the Oracle implementation was to move to a consolidated platform and a single global ERP instance. The overall ERP effort involved the following vendors and applications:

- Oracle: financial, distribution, manufacturing, and self-service purchasing

- Trilogy: product configuration
- Clarify: customer service management
- RTS and Winpeak: contract management
- GetPaid: collection package
- EaglePro: leasing
- PTC: product data management
- Mercator: legacy integration

Accenture is the system integration partner working with Oracle. The Oracle applications facilitated this aspect of the effort by integrating manufacturing support and providing an open interface architecture. This common product data architecture enabled different departments within the company to share common terminology.

EMC first produced a global prototype, mapping its business processes to the functionality of the new applications and taking advantage of new capabilities to improve the business processes. The next stage involved installation, testing, and site preparation, followed by a Big Bang go-live. EMC launched all its sites over a weekend in the fall of 2001.

In the summer of 2001, EMC began a project to deploy a single, integrated CRM solution for its customer-facing applications. Its plans focused on simplifying its current application environment, leveraging the Internet, and delivering functionality in 90- to 120-day increments. Using Oracle's rapid implementation environment, EMC was able to begin prototyping within a week of the start of the project. This environment eliminated the hardware and configuration efforts; the team was able to begin walking through the product and business processes from day one, rapidly educating the user community and facilitating configuration decisions.

EMC wanted to improve the efficiency and productivity of its sales force with a system that promoted best practices and consistent sales methods. The company wanted improved access to information on accounts, contracts, opportunities, account plans, and installed base; and it wanted forecasts in real time. Key to reaching these goals was having a single customer master database. The architecture and database were designed to support this CRM requirement.

EMC created a roadmap for moving to the entire Oracle E-Business Suite. Working with Oracle, EMC mapped business processes to application functionality. The roadmap focused on deploying logical business flows to logical user communities in short, well-defined increments.

The first phase of the implementation provided EMC's 1100 service personnel with Oracle's Professional Services Automation toolset. This toolset automates the flow from sales through project creation, time capturing, and billing to cash receipt. The initial set of processes was rolled out in less than 90 days, with incremental deployments to other users taking place every two to four weeks thereafter. The Oracle applications provide a vehicle for sharing a common platform, best practices for service personnel, and common terminology.

Hewlett-Packard

Industry	Computers/office equipment
Founded	1938
Employees	88,500
FY 2000 revenue	$48.8 billion
Market capitalization	$43.6 billion

Hewlett-Packard, the original Silicon Valley giant, is in the process of reinventing itself. A long-time focus on product and a sluggishness caused by a gradual dimming of the original vision behind the "HP Way" of doing business caused it to miss the Internet wave the first time around. While the Internet incited talk of connectivity, HP found itself with scores of product groups that didn't talk to each other. A restructuring and redirection was started in July 1999 by HP's new CEO, Carly Fiorina. Core values of creativity, initiative, and invention have been reemphasized and melded with new objectives such as collaboration, connectivity, and integration.

Creating a subsidiary from four of its divisions and redividing the core company into four new organizations has produced a revitalized and more responsive HP. Consolidating 83 independent product lines into 17 product categories allowed the company to reduce redundant overhead and to channel the savings into R&D and sales.

Products are now part of total solutions that focus on services and the customer experience. IT business and consulting have grown, as

HP provides complete solutions to companies that want to link their business transformation needs with new IT capabilities. Hewlett-Packard's vision, now restored, is that of a customer-focused provider of highly reliable and integrated business products, services, and IT infrastructure.

Looking down the information superhighway, HP believes that the Internet will evolve from a collection of Web sites that are accessed via PCs to a virtual marketplace of Internet-based "e-services" that can be invoked, on the fly, from any device. HP intends to foster this evolution of the Net by inventing a new breed of services and devices and by building the IT infrastructure needed to support billions of devices generating trillions of transactions. The company has developed a software platform called e-Speak for quickly creating and combining different kinds of online services. The platform includes the e-Speak specification, a set of programming application program interfaces (APIs) that simplifies e-service creation, and the Java-compliant e-Speak engine, which provides secure message routing across firewalls, connecting e-services to clients and to other e-services. HP offers the engine under an open-source license with the intent of establishing the e-Speak engine as an industry standard for deploying e-services.

History

Dave Packard and Bill Hewlett, fellow disciples of Fred Terman[4] and graduates of Stanford University, founded their company in 1938 in the garage of Packard's house in Palo Alto. They chose a coin from their $538 of working capital and tossed it to decide the company name. The garage is now a California State Historical Landmark.

HP's first major product was an audio oscillator. Walt Disney ordered eight of these for the production of *Fantasia*, and the company was off and running. It went public in 1957, joined the *Fortune* 500 in 1962, and built its first computer in 1966. Its first scientific handheld calculator made the slide rule obsolete in 1972. In 1986 HP introduced a family of computer systems that featured the world's first commercial

---

[4]Professor of electrical engineering and later provost at Stanford, Terman is widely considered to be *the* Father of Silicon Valley.

application of reduced-instruction-set computing (RISC) architecture, replacing complex-instruction-set computing (CISC) architecture. In the early 1990s HP pioneered a palm computing device, and in 1997 it introduced what became the industry standard for wireless interaction between computer peripherals.

In late 1998 HP began to form a subsidiary named Agilent Technologies from four HP divisions; on November 18, 1999, Agilent was listed as a public company on the New York Stock Exchange. Agilent serves the communications, electronics, life sciences, and health-care industries.

Hewlett-Packard has restructured into six organizations, three customer-facing (Business Customer Organization, Consumer Business Organization, and HP Services) and three focused on product generation (Computing Systems, Imaging and Printing Systems, and Embedded and Personal Systems). The IT Services segment is part of the Business Customer Organization. The groups collaborate closely to plan products, to create solutions, and to share important operational and financial goals. The company has more than 540 sales and support offices and distributorships in more than 120 countries worldwide.

On September 4, 2001, HP announced an agreement to buy Compaq Computer Corp. in a deal that, though strongly contested, may yet close in the first half of 2002. Compaq shareholders would receive 0.6325 share of HP stock for each Compaq share; this gave Compaq a value of $24.7 billion at the time of the announcement, but the market reacted negatively and drove the size of the deal as low as $13.4 billion before it began to recover. HP and Compaq combined would have annual revenues of some $87 billion; the joint company would be the world's largest vendor of PCs, servers, and handheld devices taken together.

Putting the Customer on the Road to E-Leadership

HP took the road to becoming an e-leader because that path led to a key corporate goal: providing world-class customer service. Greater efficiency and increased revenue are also part of the equation, and are important enough in their own rights, but improved and sustained customer relationships was an investment that the company could grow with into the next century. HP decided to begin its CRM makeover with sales force automation and to implement its solution worldwide, which meant that HP sales groups all around the globe could adopt standard ways of dealing with customers. Understanding the varying levels of enthusiasm that different cultures and business groups bring to large-scale change, HP created a CRM implementation team under Mike Overly to lead the transition and keep a finger on the pulse of the corporate-wide operation. Strong leadership and executive buy-in has been important to the success of the changeover.

The company chose a CRM solution from business partner Oracle and has deployed Oracle Sales Online globally to customer-facing employees. Customer activity is recorded in a single customer database that can be accessed by any salesperson, providing views not only into sales activity but also into activities in other organizations, such as customer contacts with the help desk, and marketing campaigns and channels directed to the customer. The ability to share information from all customer touch points was a key requirement for HP. While some processes have to be standardized, many aspects of the system can be personalized; each employee can customize the application interfaces to include specific client information and contact activities as well as data from external news sources and global financial markets. HP is also implementing Oracle's CRM marketing application, which will provide the ability to route leads automatically from marketing personnel to the internal sales staff and HP partners.

Exemplifying the collaboration enabled by the Internet, HP and Oracle have linked their sales environments, allowing the companies to work together on sales. HP and Oracle sales staff can collaborate and share data in real time over the Internet, even from within the same customer record. Both management teams enjoy expanded views into the sales pipeline and increased ability to act quickly to close deals, as well as to make more detailed global sales forecasts.

How has it worked? Forecasting is a good example. "With our rapid rate of growth, we found ourselves with seven legacy forecasting systems," said Mike Overly. "Our sales reps make commitments on what they expect to bring in every month. All of that information is then rolled up to the worldwide manager, who tries to forecast with reasonable accuracy. Unfortunately, it was impossible for the manager to push a button and get an accurate forecast or a true view of the customer. It was all done instead via word of mouth and e-mail, so it was a very disjointed process."

Singapore was the worldwide pilot for the forecasting module. Dumas Chin, BCO Sales & Marketing general manager for Singapore, said that he found the range of reports and the flexibility of the tool to be impressive. "When the overall forecast was found to be lower than expected, I was able to gain immediate visibility to unforecasted opportunities, consult with the district managers, and bring opportunities into the July forecast," Dumas reported. "I found OSO [Oracle Sales Online] particularly useful in this instance as all opportunities were in the system and could easily be retrieved."

Initial HP users in Hungary were impressed with how many—and how easily—reports could be generated. In Finland, users found that the single master database meant they no longer had to wait for long synchronizations of separate databases.

Closer to home (depending on where you live), Corporate Accounts Marketing worked with the HP sales team for Cisco Systems on an HP Day at Cisco's San Jose, California, campus. The marketing goal was to generate leads. Some 1,200 Cisco people registered for the trade-show-like event, using a Web-based registration process. "In the past, we would have had to hire a company to manage the registration process. We would get a list from them, but we never had a database or visibility by our sales reps," said Judith Fainsan-Helper, Corporate Accounts Marketing program manager. "We saved up to $5,000 by using the in-house CRM Web registration capability."

As important as the front-end savings, however, was the database created with the Web registration. Leads were qualified and prioritized by inside sales, then passed to sales reps. Sales to Cisco could be tracked to a lead generated by the HP Day event, thereby allowing the marketing ROI for that event to be measured. This hadn't been possible before.

HP next moved on to Oracle's Customer Care and Marketing applications, which will have been implemented by the time you read this. The company will have added contact management, account collaboration, and integration with other Hewlett-Packard legacy systems, directed toward meeting HP's goal of providing a customer experience that is second to none. All sales managers will be able to view up-to-the-minute sales and order information on any customer, get an accurate picture of any current service issues, and determine which marketing events the customer has recently attended.

Humana

Industry	Health care
Founded	1961
Employees	15,600
FY 2000 revenue	$10.4 billion
Market capitalization	$2.2 billion

Humana Inc. is one of the nation's largest publicly traded health services companies. The company specializes in dental, life, and disability insurance. Humana offers coverage through a variety of preferred provider organization (PPO) and health maintenance organization (HMO) plans; it also serves Medicare and Medicaid patients and members of the military.

History

In 1961 two Kentucky lawyers formed a partnership and started Extendicare, a nursing home business. By 1968 their company included seven nursing homes and was the largest nursing home chain in the United States. An initial public offering that year generated money for expansion into hospitals. The company bought its first hospital, Medical Center Hospital in Huntsville, Alabama, while the hospital was still under construction. By the time it was finished in 1970, the company owned nine other hospitals. To concentrate on its hospital business, Extendicare began selling off its nursing homes, and by 1972 it had divested itself of all 40 of its nursing homes. Extendicare changed its name to Humana in 1974 to reflect its new direction.

By 1975 Humana had 27 hospitals in the South and Southwest and was number three in the hospital business; in 1978 it bought number two, American Medicorp. By the early 1980s, Humana had become the world's largest hospital company, owning more than 80 hospitals in the United States and abroad. Among the company's innovations was a new emergency room design that ensured that critical-care patients would see a health-care professional—not an admitting clerk—on arrival.

The government began reimbursing hospitals for services to Medicare patients at fixed rates in 1983, and hospital occupancy dropped during the mid-1980s. With income down significantly, Humana responded by lowering premiums. Hospital use rose in the 1990s, but the low premiums could not cover soaring health-care costs, and profits fell. Humana decided to separate its hospital and insurance divisions. In 1993, Humana spun off its hospital operations into a new company called Galen Health Care Inc., which soon merged with Columbia/HCA.

By 1997 Humana had pulled out of a number of unprofitable markets and refocused on its core markets in the Midwest and Southeast. It bought Physician Corp. of America (PCA) and ChoiceCare, an HMO. In 1998 Humana cut back its Medicare HMO business, and in 2000 it exited the worker's compensation business altogether. In 2001 Humana bought a unit of Anthem Insurance that provides health benefits to the military.

Humana Inc. serves approximately 6.5 million members located primarily in 18 states and Puerto Rico. The company contracts with 330,000 physicians, 2,500 hospitals, and 39,000 pharmacies.

Humana Puts Health Care Online

Increasing costs and reduced payments have made cost cutting critical in the health-care industry. Humana has moved business processes such as enrollment and claims payment to the Internet, both for cost savings and as part of its business plan to transform the way it conducts business with consumers, health plan members, employers, physicians and other health-care providers, agents, and brokers. The company has invested a significant amount of capital in technological enhancements to create e-health solutions. Many transactions that health plan members, physicians, and other customers were conducting over the phone can now be done online. Using Web-based technology, Humana is expanding its business model to include providing access to valuable information that allows members to make their own health-care choices. For example, Humana has expanded its partnership with CorSolutions, a disease intervention company, to include Internet capabilities for its members. CorSolutions is now available online, enabling program members to adhere more closely to their treatment regimens and to monitor their health status on a real-time basis.

In another innovative use of the Web, Humana's pharmacy Web site now enables members to perform online searches for medication alternatives in the same therapeutic class as a given drug. This new function also provides members with estimated copayments, since costs vary from drug to drug. A drug interaction tool allows individuals to select two or more drugs and view possible interactions between the drugs. A Natural Health Encyclopedia catalogs herbal substances and supplements that are not available in the Clinical Drug Library, which is also accessible on Humana's Web site.

Humana is also applying Internet technology to its internal business processes, focusing first on sales force automation, with the ultimate goal of implementing a complete CRM solution. Humana wants all employees who interact with customers to have access to the same real-time information about prospect/customer accounts and recent activity. The Oracle applications Humana is implementing will allow its users to answer questions such as

- Which prospects currently have coverage from a specific carrier (by market, carrier, industry code, size, coverage type, or any combination of these criteria)?

- Which prospects are renewing within the next n months (by market, carrier, size, or any combination of these criteria)?

- How many prospects/leads have become quotes (by sales rep and market)?

- Which brokers or consultants are employed by prospective customers?

Managing humane care and healthy earnings is a tricky operation. In becoming an e-business, Humana has found a solution that serves both its members and its shareholders.

IKON

Industry	Business communications
Founded	1952
Employees	40,000
FY 2000 revenue	$5.4 billion
Market capitalization	$1.8 billion

IKON Office Solutions provides a broad array of business products and services for office, production, and outsourcing needs. IKON is not a manufacturer; through an international distribution and services network, it offers and supports technology from leading vendors such as Canon, Ricoh, Océ, Hewlett-Packard, Adobe, EFI, IBM, Novell, Microsoft, and Compaq. Its customers include large and small businesses, professional firms, and government agencies. IKON offerings include

Equipment: Sales, integration, and support of digital copiers, printers, and print controllers for network and production copying and printing. Color offerings include copiers and printers with a range of speeds and finishing capabilities for advanced color control and job management.

Document outsourcing: Services that blend equipment, staff, service, and supplies for on-site management of copy/print centers and mailrooms, as well as copier/printer fleet management. IKON also provides specialized document services for the legal industry, including Web-based management of highly sensitive documents. (IKON is the largest provider of legal document services in the world.)

Distributed on-demand printing: Providing customers with access to a browser-based document management, production, and distribution system via a network of digital print production centers for high-speed digital color or monochrome production, bindery/finishing services, document management, and distribution.

Imaging: Storage, conversion, and backup of paper and digital documents, including archiving and records management.

E-business development: Services provided through its e-business unit, Sysinct, IKON consultants, systems integrators, and service personnel, that offer e-business strategy development, solution architecture and design, and managed network services.

Technology training: Vendor-authorized technical training, using instructor-led, computer-based, and online training products, and consulting services.

Financing: IOS Capital, one of the largest captive finance companies in North America, is an IKON subsidiary that provides financing solutions for products and services sold by IKON.

History

Prior to its name change in January 1997, IKON Office Solutions was known as Alco Standard Corporation. Alco had functioned as a successful holding company since the 1960s, with operations in a variety of industries such as steel, gifts and glassware, food service, aerospace, paper, and office products.

By 1992, fueled by strong cash flows from its distribution businesses and strategic divestitures, Alco had become a highly focused distribution company with only two business groups: office products and paper. Strong internal growth and an aggressive acquisition program led to the rapid growth of the office products group. In 1996 the paper business was spun off as a separate publicly owned company. In 1997 Alco officially changed its name to IKON Office Solutions, Inc., to reflect the company's focus on building and expanding its office technology business. It now operates approximately 800 locations in the United States, Canada, Mexico, the United Kingdom, France, Germany, Ireland, and Denmark.

Becoming an E-Business by Design

IKON was formed through an aggressive acquisition program that targeted companies having a range of business communications capabilities, from office equipment distribution, technology services, and outsourcing to legal document production and digital printing. By the late 1990s IKON had acquired over 400 companies and was integrating a broad solution set for its customers; it was also leveraging economies of scale by making the transition from a holding company to an operating company. IKON's internal infrastructure reflected its growth by acquisition, with multiple points for customer contact and disparate internal systems.

IKON also faced radical technological change. Traditional stand-alone analog copiers were being replaced by networked digital output devices. In the competitive environment the company faced, it had to differentiate itself through its broad portfolio of integrated business communications solutions; it also had to strive increasingly to be a low-cost provider.

IKON identified the transition to an e-business platform as essential to enhancing customer service and improving operational efficiency.

The company wanted to move customer and supplier interactions to the Web. To do this, it needed to develop new business processes to exploit the Web, and it needed a solution that would integrate the company.

Specifically, IKON wanted to improve customer service and reduce costs with personalized Web-based, self-service tools for meter readings, billing, service requests, escalations, knowledge base, service histories, and service reports. The company chose Oracle as a partner to help it implement its new strategy. The choice was strongly influenced by Oracle's ability to implement end-to-end business processes with comprehensive views into all transactions and to generate detailed operational reports from these views.

IKON is installing the Oracle E-Business Suite, which includes ERP, supply chain, HRMS, and CRM applications, with heavy emphasis on contracts and service management. The software is being used to implement end-to-end processes for *Prospect to Close, Order to Cash, Procure to Pay,* and *Service.* The applications will be used by 40,000 employees, including 5,000 sales reps and 10,000 service professionals, and will manage contracts and service for over 400,000 of IKON's customers. Successful implementation will deliver a common technology and application platform, and will coordinate all data within a single instance; and it will support an increasingly mobile workforce. IKON expects to be able to provide enhanced customer service and to interact with customers through multiple channels— the Web, call center interactions, and sales and marketing.

The project sponsor is the CEO, who is supported by an executive steering committee staffed by key IKON representatives. The project has a clearly defined structure and measurable milestones. IKON expects significant increases in productivity throughout the organization, with heightened ability to monitor performance and quantify results.

JDS Uniphase

Industry	Telecom equipment
Founded	1999
Employees	14,000
FY 2001 revenue	$3.21 billion
Market capitalization	$9.5 billion

JDS Uniphase designs, develops, manufactures, and distributes a comprehensive range of advanced fiber-optic components and modules. Its products are the basic building blocks of fiber-optic networks, performing both optical-only (passive) functions such as optical-signal routing and optoelectronic (active) functions such as signal modulation.

The company's products include semiconductor lasers, high-speed external modulators, transmitters, amplifiers, couplers, multiplexers, circulators, tunable filters, optical switches, and isolators for fiber-optic applications. For its OEM customers, JDS Uniphase supplies test instruments for both system production applications and network installation. The company also designs, manufactures, and markets laser subsystems for a broad range of commercial applications, including biotechnology, industrial process control and measurement, graphics and printing, and semiconductor equipment manufacturing.

Customers of JDS Uniphase include Alcatel, CIENA, Corvis, Juniper, Lucent, Nortel, Pirelli, Scientific-Atlanta, and Tyco.

History

JDS Uniphase was formed in 1999 by a merger of JDS FITEL and Uniphase. The two telecommunications companies, though similar, had complementary product lines. JDS FITEL specialized in passive fiber-optic products such as wavelength division multiplexers, optical switches, and isolators. Uniphase Corporation was a leading manufacturer of active fiber-optic components, including lasers, modulators, and transmitters.

Uniphase had been started in 1979 by Dale Crane. He was already making helium-neon lasers in his garage, and initially his company developed and marketed gas laser subsystems to manufacturers of biomedical, industrial process control, and printing equipment. Uniphase went public in 1993 and expanded via acquisitions in the mid-1990s, which brought it into the telecommunications market. Further acquisitions included IBM's pump laser business in 1997, a maker of reflection filters used to increase the carrying capacity of a fiber-optic strand, a manufacturer of semiconductor lasers, and a maker of fiber-optic transmitters and receivers.

JDS Optics, later JDS FITEL, had been founded in 1981 by four Nortel engineers—Jozef Straus, Philip Garel-Jones, Gary Duck, and

Bill Sinclair. The company made passive fiber-optic components for routing and manipulating optical signals. JDS FITEL went public in Canada in 1996, with one of the largest IPOs in that country's history. Like Uniphase, the company expanded through acquisitions. The complementary fit of its products with those of Uniphase led to a merger, with the combined company being called JDS Uniphase.

The two companies' appetites for acquisition were also combined. In fiscal 2000 JDS Uniphase acquired ten more companies and emerged as a leading supplier of fiber-optic component and module technologies. Its timing, however, left much to be desired: while the company was rapidly scaling up, its markets were rapidly scaling down. JDSU shares dropped from a peak of $153.42 to a low of $5.12, and in July 2001 the company announced a loss for its fiscal year of $51 billion, including the largest write-off in corporate history.

The write-off means less than one might think. JDS had paid more for Uniphase, and the merged company more for its later acquisitions, than any of them was worth; but it had paid in stock that now appears to have been ridiculously overvalued, so JDSU's losses are in fact much smaller than they appear. Moreover, the terrifying drop in its share price puts the company only slightly "ahead" of major competitors, including Corning, Lucent, and Nortel, each of which declined more than 92 percent; this simply means, of course, that the fiber-optic sector was riding for a disastrous fall, as everybody now knows. Each of these four companies is likely to survive, and their futures may yet hold a lot of drama.

Rapid Response for Rapid Growth

The success of JDS Uniphase's plan for growth by rapid mergers and acquisitions was based on the execution of a comprehensive plan to integrate its acquisitions. In 1999 the existing IT infrastructure consisted of various small ERP solutions, none of which could be scaled to achieve the company's growth objectives. The company developed a long-term IT vision and implementation strategy that called for the following key components:

- ERP system from a major vendor
- A common company-wide set of data definitions and high-level business processes

- Global implementation running on a single instance
- Outsourced IT and Web-based access
- Rapid implementation

Common data definitions were developed for product, product cost, supplier, customer, chart of accounts, and employee. Process definitions were agreed upon for *Order to Cash, Recruit to Employ, Product Design to Product Release, Plan to Production,* and *Forecast to Order.* Oracle application software was selected for the rapid implementation of these definitions and business processes because it featured

- Internet architecture
- The ability to run a single, global instance
- The ability to meet requirements with an out-of-the-box solution
- High scalability

Oracle's solution was also very capable in the mixed-mode manufacturing model. A rapid deployment program was launched in partnership with KPMG Consulting to migrate all business units and acquisitions onto this standard operating model.

Thirteen sites implemented full finance, manufacturing, order management, HR, and bill of material modules, and one site implemented a partial set of modules; on average, one site went live every seventeen workdays between January 1, 2000, and November 27, 2000. All projects were completed on schedule. Over 2,200 users account for approximately $1.3 billion of JSD Uniphase revenue. By the end of 2001, twenty-nine sites, with 4,500 total users, had gone live. JDS Uniphase demonstrated the power of an ASP-supported, Web-based solution running on a high-speed Internet backbone for managing a global operation. The company believes that the flexible architecture allows it to migrate quickly from legacy systems to a new technical infrastructure at the lowest possible cost.

The JDS Uniphase sites, once implemented, initially continued to operate as separate units; but running an integrated, single-instance solution enabled the company to begin consolidating redundant operations and revising business processes based on the more complete view of its total operations that it now had. It created a shared services program to handle centrally such things as accounts payable and receivable. With many sites using the system and generating information that was easy to tap into, JDS Uniphase was able to use its data warehousing capability to look across the company and identify areas for improvement. For example, the company buys components from many vendors; the information about its purchasing practices that became available has led to more efficient buying, because agents now know (for example) when to use blanket purchase agreements and when the company can negotiate volume discounts.

"The single instance is paying off," said Joe Riera, vice president and CIO of JDS Uniphase. "The common implementation across the company is now giving us new information, new metrics, and we're using them to make improvements. Our data warehouse strategy provides for fast access to information, which in turn enables fast decisions and fast action. We put sophisticated data warehouse tools in the hands of the users so they can access any database when they want to without going through IT. This means action can be taken within minutes and hours instead of days and weeks as in the past.

"Another key component is that customers order product from all of our business units, and they obviously want one-stop shopping; they want to deal with JDS Uniphase in one common consistent fashion. By collapsing all order management into one customer service organization, we're making a quantum leap forward in presenting a single face to the customer."

Oracle

Industry	Business software
Founded	1977
Employees	42,000
FY 2000 revenue	$11 billion
Market capitalization	$91.8 billion

Oracle is the number one database software company in the world, and the number two packaged applications company. Under the guidance of CEO Larry Ellison, Oracle was the first to recognize, several years ahead of the rest of the industry, that the Internet was more than a technological phenomenon—it was a new way to do business. Ellison was quick to change Oracle's direction toward the Internet and away from client/server computing, leading the development of such things as an easily scalable Internet database (Oracle 9i), fully integrated ERP and CRM applications designed for the Internet (the Oracle E-Business Suite), and the concept, revolutionary at the time, of running all these applications globally from a single location on a single installed instance.

Ellison backed up his vision by stating that not only would Oracle run its new software in this way, it would save a billion dollars within 18 months by doing so (it actually saved $1 billion in the first year of the initiative). Originally promoted as "Oracle Eats Its Own Dog Food," the effort has become "Oracle Eats Its Own Caviar." Oracle is restructuring itself to incorporate its Internet business flows in order to maximize the benefit of using its own software. To date (as of 2001), Oracle has globally implemented Oracle Marketing Online; Oracle Sales Online, Sales Force Planning, and Incentive Compensation; Oracle iSupport, Knowledge Management, Defect and Enhancement Management, and TeleService; Oracle Partners Online; and Oracle Contracts.

Over the last several years Oracle has been able to mitigate somewhat the effects of market volatility with a continuous and substantial increase in its operating margin (33 percent in 2001). Oracle attributes this growth to the efficiency enabled by adopting sensible Internet business practices and by using its own software.

Oracle lines of business include development, sales, marketing, consulting, support, alliances, and education.[5] Oracle also has two online service organizations: Oracle On Demand is a pay-as-you-go online service that provides businesses with immediate self-service access to key business applications such as sales force automation, support services, a business-to-business (B2B) exchange, and online learning applications. The E-Business Suite Online offers that product as an online service.

Oracle's market leadership is the direct result of its technology leadership. Oracle has been number one in the relational database market since 1979. Its database market share has steadily increased, passing one-third in 2001. Its share of the application market

---

[5]Oracle University, the company's technical-education organization, is the largest such commercial enterprise in the world.

continues to grow as the importance of integration by design is recognized. Oracle is especially strong in the Internet e-business area; over 90 percent of all public dot-coms use Oracle software for their applications, databases, and application servers.

Oracle is the favored platform of application service providers. Oracle software is also run by:

- Some 65 percent of the *Fortune* 100 e-businesses
- 10 of the world's top 10 business-to-consumer (B2C) e-businesses
- 9 of the world's top 10 B2B e-businesses (all but IBM)
- More than 80 percent of all European e-businesses

History

In August of 1977, Bob Miner, Edward Oates, and Bruce Scott, sharing a single business vision, founded a small contract-programming group called Software Development Labs (SDL), which began with an initial $2,000 investment contributed by Bob Miner. Larry Ellison, who was hired soon after, is loosely considered one of the founders of the company. SDL expanded and in 1979 became Relational Software, Incorporated (RSI). RSI delivered ORACLE V.2, the world's first relational database, built using Structured Query Language (SQL).

In 1983 Ellison took over the role of president and CEO. RSI became Oracle Corporation and delivered the first portable database that ran on multiple hardware platforms. In 1987 Oracle established an applications division. A period of turbulent high-speed growth led to a corporate restructuring in 1991. Ellison refocused Oracle on reacting swiftly to customer demand and viewing things from the customer's point of view. Oracle broadened its customer support and added consulting and education organizations to its corporate footprint. In 1996 Ellison was named the *San Francisco Business Times* Executive of the Year for popularizing the network computer, a concept that became in effect the browser-based Internet application initiative that culminated with the release of the Oracle E-Business Suite 11i and Oracle 8i database in 2000.

Oracle conducts business in nearly every country on the globe; it has more than 100 operations centers in 60 countries. Revenues were $11 billion in fiscal year 2000.

Putting the *e* in Dog Food

Oracle's claim that it saved a billion dollars in a year "by eating our own dog food" provoked some understandable skepticism in the industry. It's a large claim, and the disbelieving might even think that it implies that Oracle must have been doing a lot of things wrong before. It wasn't; it was just a large international company that had grown fast and was facing the same sorts of challenges as other fast-growing companies. It was able to cut its overhead not because it fathomed the depths of the Gordian School of Business but because it executed to the simplicity of its vision of business on the Internet. As other companies convert to this new way of doing business, the savings and increased revenue will naturally follow. If believing "a billion" is difficult, just replace it with "hundreds and hundreds of millions," or whatever your company would be comfortable with, and read on. Don't try to beat complexity, or even manage it. Get rid of it. And be ready to change everything.

Even Jeff Henley, Oracle's CFO, was shocked by the amount the company had to change in order to become an e-business and by how great the benefits proved to be. "When Larry challenged the company a couple of years ago to become an e-business, I don't think any of us realized how high we could go. We've gone, in the space of a few years, from traditional low-20-percent operating margins to 35 percent. This has taken worldwide effort. Everybody, in all of our countries, and for all of our business functions, has had to fundamentally change their business processes and change the way they did business. We're using the Internet to change the way we engage and collaborate with our customers, our suppliers, and our employees."

Let's look at some of the details of where and how Oracle saved money by becoming an e-business, simplifying its business processes, and implementing a platform based on a single global instance.[6]

Marketing went through tremendous changes in both organization and process. Marketing groups had previously been divided by country and region; the groups operated somewhat independently of

---

[6]While not a technoreligion like cargo cults or Apple-ism, the main tenet of the faithful might be "a single global instance, indivisible, with information and access for all."

one another and were not always in step with sales. Marketing is now one organization with a single brand, a single consistent message, and the ability to act quickly, globally, and in communication with the other organizations that interact with the customers. Process changes have been equally significant. Seminars that were once conducted in hotels are now conducted on the Internet, and videos of the events are soon posted online for those who can't attend in person. Direct mail has been replaced by e-mail, reaching ten times more customers at a fraction of the cost. Complex product demos can now be conducted from anywhere in the world with laptops connected via the Internet to a single demonstration environment in California.

Oracle was formerly a direct sales organization. It now uses the E-Business Suite to leverage and integrate all its channels into the marketplace. Over 100 sales databases accessed by 14,000 users were combined into one database containing over 4 million records, 800,000 opportunities, and 2 million leads, spanning 64 countries and 40 currencies. Global forecasts are done weekly, monthly, and quarterly, but can be done on demand as well. Oracle's online store takes 10,000 orders a quarter, with a 75 percent labor reduction over the pre-store days. Over 6,000 sales compensation plans are completed in two weeks, versus the three to six months required before the E-Business Suite. In the first year the sales force improved its per-head margin by 67 percent. A fully integrated Campaign-to-Cash business flow has been implemented, with details of every interaction readily accessible.

E-business has allowed Oracle to reverse the support model that asserts that more products and more customers require more employees to serve them. By making more information available to the customer online and providing self-service capability, Oracle has been able to increase its customer and product base while fielding 60 percent fewer support calls.

What does all this mean? To Oracle it meant saving more than $550 million in sales, marketing, and support costs the first year these changes were in effect.

Oracle also became an e-business on the inside, in its business-to-employee (B2E) relationships. Nearly all employee and manager HR functions were automated via self-service and rules-based workflows, operating from a single global system (down from more than 70). This was no small feat, considering that Oracle has more than 42,000 employees in more than 60 countries, speaking dozens of different languages and being compensated in many different currencies. Implementing the system required a lot of work. It meant analyzing the requirements of all regions to arrive at a single data format. Where possible, business processes that varied from region to region were standardized and simplified. For example, each region had different procedures and approvals for routine employee transactions such as transfers. HR created and implemented one self-service global procedure for transfers. HR now also manages headcount, termination analysis, job definition, e-mail identification, and "reference" compensation (accounting for different currencies) on a global basis.

Oracle uses one system to support global management and reporting needs as well as local requirements and customs. HR staff can now support 80 percent more internal customers than before B2E. The overall ratio of HR staff to employees has been improved from 1:125 to 1:225; the total savings are expected to be more than $1.6 million per 10,000 employees per year. The HR budget, which used to grow at a rate approximately half that of the employee population, is now essentially flat: efficiency, not people, has accommodated the additional volume.

The goal for internal procurement was a savings of $100 million; this was attained simply by making the process self-service. For example, purchase orders and invoices are now issued online via Extensible Markup Language (XML). No longer does Oracle need an accounts payable clerk to receive an invoice and enter it into the system—and the savings that result add up quickly in a large company.

Company travel arrangements were automated and made self-service, saving 40 to 50 percent on each transaction. First-year savings were projected at $10 million, but in fact were more than $16 million. An ROI of more than $100 million is projected for the first five years.

Global IT provides perhaps the most dramatic single example of how a company can benefit by becoming an e-business. In 1998, in the client/server days of yore, Oracle spent $500 million to run its worldwide IT, requiring 1,600 people and 6.2 percent of its revenue to do so. In 2000 this function required only $263 million, about 2 percent of revenue, and only 900 people.

Savings like this become doubly important in a weak economy such as the one we've experienced since late 2000. There's no better time to increase your margins and become more efficient. And while the degree of change can be daunting, remember that savings like those described here are not one-time events. They accrue day in and day out, quarter after quarter, year after year, from the time you put e-business systems in place.

Xerox

Industry	Document management
Founded	1906
Employees	92,500
FY 2000 revenue	$18.7 billion
Market capitalization	$5.8 billion

Industry: Document Management

Like many companies, Xerox is changing from a company based on products to one based on services. The explosion of information in the 21st-century economy has put a premium on managing both data and documents. By leveraging a solid technology base, strong brand awareness, and years of studying documents and the work practices associated with them, Xerox has been reinventing itself by changing from a predominantly black-and-white-copier company into a company focusing on digital, color, and document solutions.

Xerox focuses on two primary markets: high-end production environments and digital, networked offices. Xerox and its joint-venture partner, Fuji Xerox Co. Ltd. of Japan, offer an array of document products, services, and solutions that include digital printing and publishing systems, digital multifunction devices and copiers, laser and solid ink printers, fax machines, document-management software, supplies (toner, paper, ink cartridges, etc.), and comprehensive document-management services such as running in-house production centers, developing global online document repositories, and creating networks.

Xerox offers the largest line of copiers; it also markets a broad line of digital cut-sheet and continuous-feed printers. Xerox is at the forefront of the movement from offset to digital production printing. Digital printing represents a fundamental change in the industry. Offset printing is a manufacturing-based process, with a volume-based cost model that requires mass production of static content. Digital printing is an information-based process, with a value/service model in which the size of the production run is not critical and the content can change easily. Digital capability allows Xerox to promote such e-enabled business practices as reduced inventory, on-demand printing, and easy customization.

History

Chester F. Carlson graduated from the California Institute of Technology in 1930 with a degree in physics and an interest in printing. He got his first job in the patent department of a manufacturer of electrical components. He prepared the paperwork that was submitted to the patent office, which required hours of making copies by hand—retyping manuscripts and redrawing drawings. Carlson was nearsighted and had arthritis, which made his job even more difficult. Motivated to find a better way, he began investigating automatic text and illustration reproduction on his own, working out of his apartment.

The mimeograph machine, invented by Thomas Edison, was smelly, messy, and slow, and the copies were poor. Offset printing required a photographic master, was expensive, and was not economical for low volumes. While others tried to improve these chemical or photographic processes, Carlson went in another direction—he had an idea for a reproduction technique that would use electrostatic forces to form an image in dry powder.

Years of research led in 1937 to a patent for a process he called *electrophotography*. In 1938 Carlson and an engineering friend, Otto Kornei, used photoconductivity to transfer an image from a glass slide to a metal plate with an electric charge, a bright floodlight, and sulfur powder. The image on the plate was transferred to a piece of wax paper, producing the first electrostatic copy. Over the next six years, Carlson presented his process to all the important office equipment companies, IBM and General Electric among them; it was rejected by all of them. Business executives didn't believe there was a market for a copier; carbon paper worked fine.

Undeterred by what he called "an enthusiastic lack of interest," Carlson improved his process, and in 1947 The Haloid Company, a wet-chemical photocopy machine manufacturer, bought the rights to it. Haloid changed the name from *electrophotography* to *xerography*, from the Greek *xeros* for "dry" and *graphein* for "writing."[7] Over the next 11 years The Haloid Company spent a considerable sum to develop a commercially viable xerographic machine. In 1959 the company, now called Haloid Xerox, Inc., introduced the 914, the first copier that used plain paper and was easy to use. It was an instant success. By 1961 the name *Xerox* had become synonymous with *copy*, and Haloid Xerox, Inc., became Xerox Corporation. In 1963 Xerox introduced the 813, the first desktop copier to make copies on plain paper. Xerox Corporation was one of the big business success stories of the 1960s.

A desire to diversify led Xerox into the computer business with the acquisition of Scientific Data Systems (SDS) in 1969 and the formation of the Palo Alto Research Center (PARC) in 1970. PARC became a center of innovative thinking. At the PARC facility, Xerox developed a forward-looking networked personal computer called the Alto and a host of other computing ideas and designs that are now taken for granted: multitasking, bit-mapped screens, Ethernet local area networks, WYSIWIG word processing, the laser printer, the mouse, and the graphical user interface (GUI).[8]

The early 1970s saw Xerox embroiled in legal troubles over its business practices. It was spending millions on antitrust court cases and losing more millions on its computer business. Xerox shut down SDS and reported its first quarterly decline in profits since 1960. Internal critics of the company's involvement in computers became more vocal, and Xerox missed the opportunity to market the Alto—focusing instead on a dedicated word processor, an idea whose time was quickly passing.

In 1981 Xerox introduced PARC's next computing product, the Star office system, an advanced, networked, mouse-driven, WYSIWIG electronic publishing system with remote storage and a laser printer. The Star system was easy to learn and use: It had a now-standard GUI

[7]The Haloid Company trademarked the word *Xerox* in 1948.

[8]The graphical user interface was demonstrated for Steve Jobs and later became the basis for the Apple Macintosh in 1984.

consisting of icons, menus, and windows. In many ways ahead of its time, it was sold by a copier sales staff that didn't understand it; it was wrong for the market; and it had some flaws, such as being a closed system. The IBM PC was introduced about the same time, and the idea of *personal computing* took off, somewhat at the expense of PARC's concept of distributed networked computing. Cheaper and simpler, if less capable, alternatives doomed the Star. Of the many good ideas to come out of PARC, only the laser printer made it to market. Disillusioned, many of PARC's gifted researchers left, some to found their own companies, like Bob Metcalfe with 3Com Corporation and Chuck Geschke and John Warnock with Adobe Systems. Xerox began extracting itself from the computer market.

In the 1990s Xerox moved away from data processing and personal computers to focus more on document production and management. To emphasize this change in direction, in 1994 it adopted a new logo and corporate signature—The Document Company, Xerox.

Xerox is now number one in digital copiers for the third year in a row, accounting for nearly one in three U.S. black-and-white digital copiers placed in 2000, according to estimates by Gartner Dataquest.

Xerox distributes its products in the Western Hemisphere through divisions and wholly owned subsidiaries. In Europe, Africa, the Middle East, and parts of Asia including Hong Kong, India, and China, Xerox distributes through Xerox Limited and related companies. Fuji Xerox Co., Limited, an unconsolidated entity jointly owned by Xerox Limited and Fuji Photo Film Company Limited, develops, manufactures, and distributes document-processing products in Japan and other areas of the Pacific Rim, Australia, and New Zealand.

Rapid Response from Front Office to Back

Xerox has a history of technical expertise and in-house solutions. As the company expanded in size and geographic reach, this led to significant segmentation in process and information flow. The company had a culture that supported one-off systems and independent operation. As a result, for example, sales groups did not share customer information and were not aware of outbound marketing campaigns or billing inconsistencies. There could be many separate records for the same customer; it was impossible for Xerox to present the same face to every customer, or even to recognize one customer as the same at different times or through different channels. On top of this, managing all the disparate systems required a significant chunk of revenue.

Xerox also had an understanding of the power of information and the gains that it could attain by changing its business model to an e-business model. With goals that included sharing customer information, presenting a single face to the customer, and Web-enabling the sales process to increase the efficiency and reduce the cost of sales, Xerox decided on integrated software from Oracle Corporation that included both front-office and back-office applications. Of special interest to Xerox was the new ability to coordinate multiple sales channels, from marketing campaigns to taking orders, with sales reps being paid on every transaction along the way.

For example, Xerox Omnifax has been able to automate its entire business process, from sales to order fulfillment and invoicing, as well as all back-office accounting functions. Financials can be tracked on one automated system. Orders can be tracked from booking to shipping, and rental returns can be tracked in inventory. Xerox is leveraging the Internet as its own global network.

Acronym Glossary

A/P: Accounts payable

A/R, AR: Accounts receivable

AA&D: Aviation, aerospace, and defense

ABC: Activity-based cost(s)

AD: Airworthiness Directive

ADSL: Asynchronous Digital Subscriber Line

AIDS: Acquired immune deficiency syndrome

AMA: American Medical Association

ANSI: American National Standards Institute

APAC: Asia and Pacific

API: Application programming interface

ASP: Application service provider

ATP: Available to promise

B2B: Business-to-business

B2C: Business-to-consumer

B2E: Business-to-employee

BC4J: Business Components for Java

BIS: Business intelligence systems

BOM: Bill of materials

BPR: Business process reengineering

BSS: Business support system(s)

CAD: Computer-aided design

CAM: Computer-aided manufacturing

CATV: Community antenna (cable) television

CD: Compact disk

CEO: Chief executive officer

CFO: Chief financial officer

CFR: Contact Flight Rule

CIO: Chief information officer

CISC: Complex-Instruction-Set Computing

CLEC: Competitive local exchange carrier

COA: Chart of accounts

COGS: Cost of goods sold

CPFR: Collaborative planning for forecasting and replenishment

CPG: Consumer packaged goods

CPU: Central processing unit

CRM: Customer relationship management

CSR: Customer service representative

CUSIP: Committee on Uniform Security Identification Procedures

D&B: Dun & Bradstreet

DJIA: Dow Jones Industrial Average

DoC: (U.S.) Department of Commerce

DSL: Digital Subscriber Line

DSO: Days' sales outstanding

DTC: Direct-to-consumer

E&Y: Ernst & Young

EDI: Electronic Data Interchange

EDIFACT: Electronic Data Interchange for Administration, Commerce, and Trade

EDMS: Enterprise data management system

EFT: Electronic funds transfer

ELA: Equipment Leasing Association

EMEA: Europe, Middle East, and Africa

EOQ: End of quarter

ERP: Enterprise resource planning

F/A: Fixed assets

FAA: (U.S.) Federal Aviation Administration

FAQ: Frequently asked question

FDA: (U.S.) Food & Drug Administration

FSI: Financial services industry *or* institution

FSR: Field sales representative

FTC: (U.S.) Federal Trade Commission

FY: Fiscal year

GAAP: Generally accepted accounting principles

GATT: General Agreement on Trade and Tariffs

GEPS: GE Power Systems

GL: General ledger

GUI: Graphical user interface

HASP: Hub-and-spoke pattern

HMO: Health maintenance organization

HR: Human resources

HRMS: Human resources management system

HTML: Hypertext Markup Language

HTTP: Hypertext Transfer Protocol

IDC: International Data Corporation

IFR: Instrument Flight Rule

IND: Investigational new drug

IP: Internet Protocol

IPO: Initial public offering

IRS: (U.S.) Internal Revenue Service

iSD: (Oracle's) Internet Sales Division

ISP: Internet services provider

IT: Information technology

IXC: Interexchange carrier

JDBC: Java Database Connectivity

JSP: Java Server Pages

KPI: Key performance indicator

LAN: Local area network

LATA: Local Access and Transport Area

LOB: Line of business

MIX: Multimedia Internet exchange

MRI: Magnetic resonance imaging

MRO: Maintenance, repair, and overhaul

MRP: Material requirements planning

MTBF: Mean time between failures

MTTR: Mean time to repair

NAS: Network-attached storage

NASDAQ: National Association of Securities Dealers Automated Quotation (system)

NIAP: National Internet Access Program

NYSE: New York Stock Exchange

OAG: Open Applications Group (, Inc.)

OC: Optical carrier

OEM: Original equipment manufacturer

OFDM: Oracle Financial Data Manager

OM: Order management

OMO: Oracle Marketing Online

OPM: Oracle Process Manufacturing

OS: Operating system

OS/2: (IBM's) Operating System/2

OSI: Oracle Sales Intelligence

OSO: Oracle Sales Online

OSS: Operational support system(s)

P/E: Price/earnings

PARC: (Xerox's) Palo Alto Research Center

PBM: Pharmaceutical benefit management

PC: Personal computer

PDA: Personal digital assistant

PL/SQL: Procedural Language/Structured Query Language

PO: Purchase order

PPO: Preferred provider organization

PRM: Partner relationship management

QA: Quality assurance

QTD: Quarter to date

R&D: Research and development

RAID: Redundant array(s) of inexpensive disks

RFQ: Request for quotation

RISC: Reduced-instruction-set computing

RMA: Returned merchandise authorization

ROI: Return on investment

ROLAP: Relational online analytical processing

SAN: Storage area network

SCM: Supply chain management

SFA: Sales force automation

SKU: Stock-keeping unit

SONet: Synchronous optical network

SQL: Structured Query Language

SR: Service request

SRDF: (EMC's) Symmetrix Remote Data Facility

SSD: Solid-state disk

SSL: Secure Sockets Layer

SVGA: Super Video Graphics Array

SVP: Senior vice president

TCA: (Oracle's) Trading Community Architecture

TCO: Total cost of ownership

TPR: Temporary price reduction

UI: User interface

UK: United Kingdom

UN: United Nations

UOM: Unit of measure

URL: Uniform Resource Locator

USD: U.S. dollars

USPS: United States Postal Service

VAD: Value-added distributor
VAN: Value-added network
VDSL: Voice over Digital Subscriber Line
VFR: Visual Flight Rule
VoIP: Voice over Internet Protocol
VP: Vice president
VPD: Virtual private database
VPN: Virtual private network
WAP: Wireless Application Protocol
WTC: World Trade Center
WWW: World Wide Web
WYSIWIG: What you see is what you get
XML: Extensible Markup Language
Y2K: Year-2000
YTD: Year to date

Index

Note: Locators in **bold** indicate additional display material.